A GREAT WEEKEND IN

AMSTERDAM

A GREAT WEEKEND IN
AMSTERDAM

Wherever you are in Europe, it's never more than an hour or so by plane to Amsterdam, and it would be a real shame not to seize your next chance to spend a few days in the city they call the 'Venice of the North', the 'city of tulips', the 'city of a hundred canals', the 'diamond capital' or the 'city of the golden century'. But, clichés aside, Amsterdam is like nowhere else. Just don't expect to find any buxom blondes in clogs with a gouda cheese under one arm and a bunch of tulips under the other. The city's many faces are as varied as its districts which, though close in space, are all quite unique.

Amsterdam is a paradoxical place, conservative in some ways, pioneering in many others. This home of right-thinking Calvinists was the first city to establish a trade union for prostitutes, pass draconian laws against pollution from cars and legalise marriage between people of the same sex. Amsterdam's coffee-shops, where the sale and consumption of cannabis resin is permitted, and its highly mixed and apparently mutually accepting population of 145 different nationalities reflect the city's tolerant attitudes.

If there's one thing all Amsterdammers share, it's a love of trade, which sends them all over the world to bring back the rare objects you find in the big antique shops on Spiegelstraat or the Rokin. But the city also has dozens of junk shops, which are fun to explore and where you might find a bargain.

Take advantage of your trip to buy all your bulbs or hunt down the last word in gadgets in the Jordaan district. You can buy cheap clothes here too, as long as you're not expecting the elegance of Paris or Milan.

Don't panic! With only 730,000 inhabitants – and 550,000 bicycles – Amsterdam is still a small city, enclosed by a network of canals linked to the North Sea. You can get around it easily on foot, from patrician houses to 'brown cafés', losing yourself in places that look like a Van Goyen seascape or a genre painting by Jan Steen. It's then that you begin to understand why Amsterdammers use the word *gezellig* so often. This is an untranslatable word that is often used to convey the conviviality of their relaxed surroundings. It doesn't take a moment for Amsterdam's love of partying to turn the street into a carnival full of fauns in pointed hats, purple-haired punks and young men swathed in leather. After you've watched one of these spontaneous shows, spent some time admiring Rembrandt's painting of *The Night Watch* and Van Gogh's *Sunflowers* and are at last leaning on the counter of one of the city's 1,402 cafés or dancing in a club's hypnotic lights, you'll know you've touched the beating heart of Amsterdam.

On your way out of the city, having glimpsed its true face, stammered out a few words in Dutch, tasted some of the thousand subtle flavours of *jenever*, watched one of the forty shows on offer every day of the week, rifled through all the market stalls and been to every museum, there'll only be one thing left you know you really have to do, and that's come back to Amsterdam.

How to get there

Spring and summer are probably the best seasons to get the most out of your weekend trip to Amsterdam, but you can never be absolutely certain of getting the better of the Dutch climate. In practice, it may be rainy and cold at any time of year.

July and August are not only the hottest months (21-26°C/ 70-79°F), they're also the period when most hotels charge low season prices. And if you can cope with bitterly cold, damp weather, Amsterdam is quite charming in the depths of winter, when the frozen canals recall the work of the great 17th-century painters.

HOW TO GET THERE

Since cars are completely useless in Amsterdam, the quickest and most comfortable way to travel is by plane.

BY PLANE

If you're only going for a short break, take all your things with you in the cabin as hand luggage. This will allow you to check in at the last minute, half an hour before your flight. For luggage to go in the hold, 23kg/50lbs is the permitted maximum in economy class and 30kg/66lbs in business class. If you go

BY TRAIN

You can get the train to Amsterdam from any major city in Europe.

The Eurostar offers a fast service direct from London to Brussels or Paris where you can transfer to Amsterdam. For more information call Eurostar on ☎ 0990 186 186 or European Rail on ☎ 020 7387 0444.

From Paris, the SNCF offers a very efficient service to Amsterdam. You can check their website www.sncf.fr or call them on ☎ 0033 836 35 35 39 (Calls are taken in English).

over the limit you'll have to pay a surcharge calculated per kilo.

FLIGHTS FROM THE UK

Seven major carriers fly to Schiphol airport from the UK and Ireland including:

British Airways
www.british-airways.com
☎ 0345 222 111
Daily direct flights from the UK to Amsterdam.

British Midland
www.britishmidland.com
☎ 0345 554 554
Offers two flights daily.

KLM
www.klm.com
☎ 08705 074 074
Flies to Amsterdam from many locations in Europe. Check website or phone for schedules.

FROM IRELAND

Aer Lingus
www.aerlingus.ie
☎ 01 886 8888
Daily flights from Dublin and Cork.

FROM THE USA AND CANADA

KLM
www.klm.com
☎ 1 800 221 2000
Offer daily code-share service with Northwest Airlines from major airports.

Delta
www.delta-air.com
☎ 1 800 241 4141
Offers daily code-share flights direct to Amsterdam from major airports

TWA
www.twa.com
☎ 1 800 221 2000
Offers daily direct flights to Amsterdam.

Air Canada
www.aircanada.com
☎ 1 800-555-1212
Flies to Amsterdam daily via London.

INCLUSIVE BREAKS

Tour operators generally offer 2 or 3 day weekend breaks at fixed prices including transport (plane, train or coach) and various categories of hotel. You can also contact some tour operators directly. The Amsterdam Travel Service (☎ 01992 456056, UK) and City Escapades (☎ 020 8563 8959, UK) can plan your itinerary, including flights, hotels and excursions. Alternatively you can check current deals on the internet: **Expedia** (www.expedia.com) and the **Travel Shop** (www.the-shopping-centre. com/travel) provide general travel information as well as offers on city breaks.

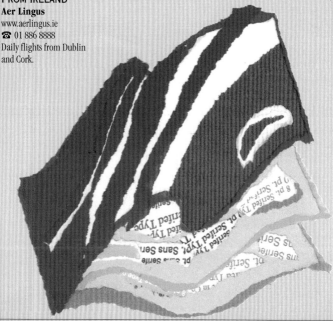

FROM AUSTRALIA AND NEW ZEALAND

KLM offers direct flights from major Australian airports to Amsterdam, but it may be cheaper to find a flight with a stopover. From New Zealand you can fly with **Qantas** via Sydney, and **New Zealand Air** and **KLM** offer a codeshare service via Los Angeles. It is worth seeing a travel agent to work out the cheapest and most convenient route.

KLM
www.klm.com
☎ 1 800 505 7474 Freephone (Australia)
☎ 093 09 17 82 (New Zealand)
KLM offers a direct code-share service to Amsterdam from Sydney and a code-share service via LA from New Zealand

Qantas
www.qantas.com
☎ 13 13 13 (from anywhere in Australia)
☎ 09 357 8900/ 0800 808 767 (New Zealand)
Qantas offers daily flights from Sydney to Amsterdam via London, Frankfurt or Singapore. From New Zealand you will have to fly via Sydney.

British Airways
www.british-airways.com
☎ 02 8904 8800 (Australia)
☎ 09 356 8690 (New Zealand)
Offers daily flights from major Australian airports via London Heathrow.

FROM THE AIRPORT TO THE CENTRE OF AMSTERDAM

Schiphol airport is 18km/11 miles southwest of Amsterdam. You have a choice of three modes of transport to take you to the city centre. Quickest and fastest is the train, which gets you to Amsterdam's central station in 20mins. Departures every 10mins until 12.30am and every hour between 1am and 6am, from the airport station located under the terminal. Ticket offices are open day and night (6Fl one way, 10.25Fl return).

A KLM bus to six of Amsterdam's grand hotels leaves the airport's main exit every half hour between 6.30am and 6pm. Buy your ticket from the driver, price 17.50Fl.

You can get a taxi from the airport to your hotel door for about 60Fl. Journey time varies from 30mins to 1 hour.

CUSTOMS

As signatories to the Schengen agreement, the Dutch do not make systematic customs checks at their borders on nationals of the European Union. If you enter the country by car from Belgium, you won't even notice. If you're travelling by train, however, your luggage may be searched by French or Belgian customs officials because of the drugs traffic. So beware: although possession of 5gm/1.5oz of marijuana is permitted in the Netherlands, it's entirely illegal once you cross the border. Permitted duty-free purchases are: 200 cigarettes or 50 cigars, 2 litres of wine, 1 litre of alcohol of more than 22°, 2 litres of less

than 22°, 50cl of perfume, 25cl of eau de toilette and 500gm/1.1lbs of coffee, but don't forget that duty-free is only available between Amsterdam and non-EU countries, following the abolition of

duty-free between EU countries in June 1999. The import of firearms, amunition, knives, swords, etc. is illegal.

RENTING A CAR

Unless you're intending to tour the country around Amsterdam, a car will just be a source of problems. There are very few hotels with a free car park and you'll spend a fortune on parking meters (5Fl per hour) if you want to avoid getting your car clamped. The city is comparatively small and public transport runs all night so you're really better off leaving the car at home. However, if you can't bear to be without your own wheels and are at least 21 years old, you'll be better off renting a car.. You can arrange this from home, otherwise the car rental offices at Schiphol (open from 6am to 10.30pm) are in the Arrivals lounge between Central and West. E.

Europcar offers the best weekend rates. ☎ 31 3164 190 (Amsterdam); www.europcar.com.

CASH AND BUDGETING

The Dutch currency is the guilder *(gulden)*, which is divided into a hundred cents. The notes come in denominations of 10, 25, 50, 100, 250 and 1,000 guilders. The coins are worth 5Fl, 2.5Fl, 1Fl, 25 cents *(kwartje)*, 10 cents *(dubbeltje)* and 5 cents *(stuiver)*. There are no restrictions on the import and export of Dutch currency by non-residents.

It's better to buy your guilders at home before you leave. In Amsterdam, the banks are shut at the weekend and the bureaux de change charge 2.25-3% commission plus a 5-7.5Fl fee per transaction, so watch out. The GWK has branches open round the clock at Schiphol airport and the Centraal Station, and these will change notes and traveller's cheques at reasonable rates. American Express (Damrak, 66 and Van Baerlestraat, 39, 9am-5pm) also charges low commission

rates. There are also a great many cash machines where you can use a credit or debit card to withdraw money directly if it's part of an international network (Visa, Diner's, Mastercard or American Express).

Most upmarket shops and restaurants accept credit cards, but many smaller ones don't. If you want to carry large sums of money, it's better to take traveller's cheques.

Life in Amsterdam can be expensive. You should expect to pay 30-60Fl for a meal, 5-12.5Fl to go to a museum, 3Fl for a tram ticket, 3-5Fl for a coffee or a beer, 10-20Fl to get into a discotheque, and 20-45Fl for a ticket for the theatre or a concert. After paying for your room and transport you should allow 300-400 Fl spending money.

Of course, if you're travelling on a student budget, Amsterdam is still very much within your reach: you can get something to eat and a place to stay for very little, though in conditions that can only be

HEALTH CARE

If you're following a course of medical treatment, make sure you take enough medication with you to cover the time you'll be away, as you can't be sure of finding it in Amsterdam. EU citizens are entitled to free medical assistance (covering the cost of treatment and medication), from doctors approved by the A.N.O.Z. (Algemeen Nederlands Onderling Ziekenfonds), on presentation of an E111 form, which is provided on request in advance of travel by your national sickness insurance provider. You can obtain an E111 from your post office.

You may be surprised to see the many very well-stocked chemist's shops in Amsterdam that sell everything from toothpaste and hair-care products to sun-screen, vitamins, food supplements and some medicinal items that you might expect to obtain from a pharmacist.

described as spartan. But however much you have to spend, the enormous choice of hotels and restaurants means that you'll always be able to find a room and a meal to suit your wallet.

THINGS TO LOOK FOR IN AMSTERDAM

Amsterdam is the city of diamonds, antiques, books and curiosities, so if you're looking to buy any of these things, you'll find there are some very good bargains to be had.

Many gadgets, items for the home, off-the-peg clothes and accessories are attractively priced and you'll often find items here that you can't get elsewhere.

Generally speaking, Dutch fashions tend to follow the broad trends of the Anglo-Saxon countries and you'll find jersey, vinyl and other synthetic materials rather than natural linens and raw silk.

FORMALITIES

Nationals of countries in the European Union, including children under 16, must have a valid identity card or passport. A passport that has expired within the last five years is also acceptable. If you're travelling from the U.S.A, Canada, Australia or New Zealand you will require a valid passport. You will only require a visa if you are staying for three months or longer.

INSURANCE

The fixed insurance deals offered by tour operators usually include cover for cancellation or lost or stolen luggage. Provided you pay for your plane or train ticket by credit card, you're usually entitled to good cover for medical expenses and the cost of repatriation, but do check the extent of the cover offered with your credit card company before you go. If you make the bookings yourself, it's always a good idea to take out cover for the cost of repatriation with an accredited insurance company.

LOCAL TIME

Amsterdam is one hour ahead of Greenwich Mean Time, 6 hours ahead of the U.S.A and Canada (Eastern Standard Time), 8 hours behind Australia (East Coast) and 10 hours behind New Zealand.

VOLTAGE

In the Netherlands, the current is 220 volts. It is handy to bring an adaptor, as Holland has two-way plugs and sockets, not three.

USEFUL SOURCE

Netherlands Tourist Office (VVV)

The VVV, the national tourist organisation, has three offices in Amsterdam and is the most reliable place to find information about accommodation, events and excursions (see page 35).

If you want to find out information before you leave home, the NBT (Netherlands Board of Tourism) has several offices abroad.

UK ☎ 020 7828 7900
USA ☎ 212 370 7360
Canada ☎ 416 363 1557

You can also check what will be going on when you get there by looking on NBT's website, www.goholland.co.uk.

REFLECTIONS OF THE GOLDEN AGE

In the 17th century Amsterdam became one of Europe's most flourishing capitals, thanks to the success of its traders and the freedom of thought permitted there. The city welcomed exiles from all sides and doubled in size in ten years. Meanwhile, the wealthy merchants of the prestigious Dutch East India Company were challenging the Portuguese monopoly of the spice trade.

▲ *John Calvin, 16th century wood engraving.*

and also to develop local industries, such as brewing, silk-manufacture, diamond-cutting, printing, map-making and ship-building.

'In this great city where, other than myself, there is not a single man who is not engaged in trading goods, everyone is so occupied attending to his profit that I could stay here for the rest of my life without ever being seen by anyone.'
René Descartes, 1631.

THE CALVINIST CREED

'Let us take the gain that comes to us as though it were from the hand of God.' With advice like that John Calvin was bound to appeal to the merchants of Amsterdam, who abandoned the teachings of the Spanish Catholics and welcomed many refugees, guaranteeing them both economic freedom and the freedom to think and worship as they chose.

ECONOMIC AND RELIGIOUS LIBERALISM

The vast influx of foreign capital made it possible to fund major maritime expeditions

A CITY WITHOUT PALACES

The only aim the rich Calvinists had in making money was to hoard their wealth. They were not interested in ostentatious splendour, or palaces, so there's no architecture worthy of the Golden Age. All you'll find are a few decorative masks

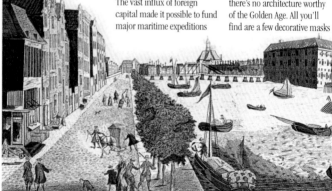

Frans Hals : *The Archers' Banquet*

and grotesque figures to enliven the modest gabled façades of brick. And because tax was assessed by the *'kavel'*, or plot of building land with a width of 7.35m/8yds and a depth of 60m/65yds, few people risked building on much larger plots.

EARLY TOWN PLANNING

To house a population that had tripled in forty years, it was decided to enlarge the city by digging three new canals, the Herengracht, the Keizersgracht and the Prinsengracht, around the port and the old quarters. The city was built all in one go and owes its harmonious quality to the rules imposed by the local council, which specified not only what materials could be used and the dimensions of the houses, but also located their inhabitants according to their social status, work or origins.

THE BIRTH OF BOURGEOIS ART

Freed from the yoke of religion, Dutch painters diversified into genres which reveal the material concerns of their wealthy bourgeois patrons. Commissions for single and group portraits came flooding into the studios of well-known painters such as Rembrandt and Frans Hals. Pictures of

Gerrit Dou : *Woman with Dropsy*

landscapes or simple church interiors were successful in a way unheard-of elsewhere. However these highly realistic

depictions express a strict protestant morality – tavern scenes portray the evils of the excessive consumption of alcohol and tobacco, while the withered flowers of the still lifes are reminders of the vanity of worldly wealth and pleasures.

A DIFFERENT IMAGE OF REMBRANDT

Rembrandt van Rijn's real name was *Rembrandt Harmenszoon*, meaning, 'Rembrandt, son of Harmen'. He married in 1634, but then took his children's nanny as his mistress. However in 1649 this woman left him and took him to court for breaking his promise to marry her. The painter then took on a young serving girl, Hendrickje Stoffels, who became his companion. However this behaviour was considered scandalous because Rembrandt's fame was such that he was regarded as a public figure. The Dutch Reformed Church condemned and reprimanded him and the unfortunate Hendrickje was also banned from taking Holy Communion. The puritanical public turned against the artist, who later died in disgrace.

THE SEEDS OF MODERNISM

Turning its back on the floral exuberance of Art Nouveau, which was all the rage in France and Belgium, Holland favoured a more rational form of architecture, which exploited the potential of emerging industrial techniques. The priority in Amsterdam, as in other places, was to use objects and furniture as a way of bringing art into daily life. In this way the modern look came into being.

THE NEW AESTHETIC CREED

The 'Arts and Crafts' exhibition held in London in 1880 marked the dawn of a new aesthetics which was to have an important influence on Dutch artists, particularly since Holland's Germanic culture tends to favour severity over excess. The cult of the pure line and geometrical shapes acted as the vehicle of a new art form which gradually evolved towards Expressionism.

FUNCTIONALISM

H. P. Berlage was an important figure of the avant garde because of the way he exploited the qualities of old and new materials in functional ways.

With his monumental building for the Amsterdam stock exchange (1898-1903), he succeeded in constructing a simple, sober structure of glass and steel, without any form of ornamentation, standing on the building of brick and stone.

THE AMSTERDAM SCHOOL

The socialist city council built affordable housing in south Amsterdam for the new working class. Rationalism and progress were the watchwords. However, the

'Dageraad' complex, designed between 1921 and 1923 by Michael de Klerk and P.L. Kramer, seems more fantastical than rational in conception. Expressionist ideas about movement are here rather playfully reflected in undulations, sudden vertical constructions and the interplay of different colours.

THE DE STIJL MOVEMENT

Founded in Leiden in 1917 by Theo van Doesburg, the De Stijl movement, whose best

Robert Dusarduyn, a former theatre designer, has been specialising in collecting Art Deco objects and furniture since 1972. His collection of velvets from the Amsterdam School is well worth seeing.
Molsteeg, 5 and 7
Open Fri. 12.30-7pm
and Sat. 11.30am-6pm
or by appointment.
☎ 623 21 89.

MODERNISM AND DAILY LIFE

The rigorously orthogonal forms he gave to his creations link Gerrit Rietveld (1888-1964) firmly to the De Stijl movement. The famous red and blue armchair, which he designed in 1919, marks the beginning of the era of simple furniture which could be mass-produced. Later he developed ever-more purified forms, which have influenced the work of many of today's designers.

ART DECO

This catch-all term, first used during the 1925 Paris International Exhibition, covers the very varied artistic production of the first half of the 20th century.

The furniture and objects made from 1915 onwards reflect a return to styles from the past, with massive forms, contrasting colours, geometrical decoration and the use of glass and steel. The use of rare materials (lacquer, skin, ivory) made this a luxury

style of limited production. The category of Art Deco covers both Rietveld's Cubist table and the comfortable 'Vanity Fair' armchair.

representative is Piet Mondrian, evolved out of neo-Plasticism. This was a theory of painting characterised by the rigorous use of very simple means of expression, such as horizontal and vertical lines, in combination with evenly-applied primary colours. Sometimes black and white would also be included, either as pure colours or mixed.

A PIONEER OF ABSTRACT ART

Mondrian, whose early influences were Toorop and Seurat, is regarded as one of the pioneers of abstract art. He made a profound impression on all of contemporary western art, both through his pictures (*Composition in red, yellow and blue* and *Victory Boogie-Woogie*, among others) and his writings, such as the *De Stijl Manifesto*, *The Triptych of Evolution* or *Natural Reality and Abstract Reality*.

Art Deco lamp at Robert Dusarduyn's gallery

LIBERTY AND LIBERTINES

Since the 17th century, Amsterdam has been known for its tolerance. Though their apparently lax attitudes have often been criticised by their European neighbours, the Dutch uphold the right to true freedom of action and thought. In Holland differences are accepted, whether a person is foreign, or homosexual, drops out of society or rejects moral conventions. Holland was also first to legalise abortion, allow euthanasia and decriminalise soft drugs.

SQUATTING, AN OUTDATED PHENOMENON

In the early 1970s it was fairly easy for a student to find free accommodation in a magnificent residence on the Herengracht. The *provos'* (see right) action to combat property speculation was more or less permitted by the city council, which preferred to see such buildings occupied before renovation. In what can only be seen as a sign of the times, the new housing law passed in 1986 put an end to this practice.

THE *PROVOS*, GENTLE ACTIVISTS

In 1964 a group of young protesters describing themselves as non-violent ecologists against the status quo launched a series of amusing stunts known as 'happenings'. They met at the Dam and advocated non-polluting cars, the right to social housing and sexual freedom. These gentle subversives succeeded in getting elected on to Amsterdam's city council, where they instigated the anti-car policies in force today.

COFFEE-SHOPS

The cannabis culture was set in motion by Kees Hockert,

who, in 1961, discovered a loophole in the penal code that made it illegal to possess dried cannabis flowers but not to grow them. Although it's still a crime to possess soft drugs, the Dutch government permits the sale of cannabis resin in Amsterdam's three hundred or so coffee-shops. However the amount allowed for sale was recently reduced from 30gm/approx. 1oz to 5 gm/approx. 0.2oz).

BUSINESS AND THE LIMITS OF PERMISSIVENESS

Recently the council of Delfzijl, a small town on the northern coast of the Netherlands, not far from Groningen, closed down all the local coffee-shops and opened a new one, which is run by a council employee. Not a bad way to keep a discreet eye on the customers and help balance the budget!

LOVE IN A SHOP WINDOW

Like any other port, Amsterdam has its prostitutes. The difference is that here there's none of the hypocrisy to be found in other countries – the prostitutes are on display in shop windows. Brothels are officially licensed and these ladies of easy virtue pay tax. In the final analysis it's a natural way of recognising their profession – which is, after all, the oldest in the world – and preventing them from touting for business on the streets, a practice which is still illegal in Holland.

GAY CITY

After San Francisco, Amsterdam is the city with the highest number of gay clubs and bars in the world. It's the only country in Europe where homosexual couples can marry and where they have the right to raise children. The gay community has a newspaper called the *Gay Krant*, and a centre for the protection of its rights. It also has an official 'pink day' in the holiday calendar.

POTTERY

Among the precious cargoes brought back from the east by the ships of the Dutch East India Company was the famous blue-and-white porcelain from China. The first auction in 1604 caused enormous excitement among the Dutch bourgeoisie, whose dream it was to own such things. Chinese porcelain was expensive because of its rarity and was soon copied in the factories of Delft, which doubled in number between 1651 and 1665.

A TECHNIQUE FROM ITALY

The use of faience was introduced to the Netherlands in the early 16th century by Italian potters who had established workshops in Antwerp. At this time kitchen equipment for daily use was made either of tin, wood or skin, following Germanic tradition. Politico-religious conflicts drove the Italian potters to migrate to the northern provinces, where they founded factories in Delft, Makkum, The Hague and Haarlem.

DELFT FAIENCE

The terms porcelain and faience are often confused. In fact, although the factories of Delft and Makkum began to concentrate on producing copies of Chinese porcelain in

1613, Dutch factories have never made anything but white faience, decorated either in monochrome blue or a combination of colours. White Delftware pieces intended for kitchen use haven't been made for a very long time and are highly sought-after.

PORCELAIN OR FAIENCE ?

In porcelain fired at high temperatures (1,350°C/2,880°F), the china clay (kaolin) and the glaze form a highly resistant amalgam without flaws. Porcelain is very thin and translucent. Faience is made from a different kind of clay and is fired twice. After the first firing the earthenware object is covered in an opaque, white, tin-based enamel, and may be decorated or not. The piece is then fired again at 800°C. Faience is less solid

HOW TO RECOGNISE REAL DELFTWARE

Beware! Not all blue-and-white ceramics are Delftware. Souvenir-sellers may not scruple to inscribe the underside of ceramics made in Taiwan with the royal crown and, beneath it, the magic words *'Köninklijk Delftsblauw'*. The first clue to the authenticity of your piece is the price. To be certain, however, you should make sure that you buy your Delftware from specialist shops, particularly if you're looking for antique pieces, and always check that they have the proper mark.

than porcelain and may also have flaws, such as bubbles caused by firing at too high a temperature or the seeping of the decoration into the enamel. Delft faience has a second coating (transparent glaze) which heightens the colours. And in case you didn't know, the word 'faience' comes from the name of the Italian town of Faenza, where this technique was developed in the 15th century.

MAKKUM FAIENCE

Though less well-known by the general public, the royal factory at Makkum is the oldest in the Netherlands. It was founded in 1594 and since 1674 has been owned by the same family, the Tichelaars, who, from generation to generation, have passed down the secrets of the enamels that give the pieces made by their factory their particular beauty. The blue monochrome or multi-coloured decoration is always

hand-done by skilled craftspeople and is more delicate than that of Delft.

DE PORCELEYNE FLES

Most of the Delft factories closed their doors around 1742 as a result of competition from English and French products. The only factory to have maintained continuous production since it was founded in 1653 is the 'De Porceleyne Fles' factory. King Willem III gave it the title of royal factory in order to stimulate its declining output. Today this and the Makkum factory are the only ones to produce real Delftware, which is authenticated by a mark on the underside of the object.

HOLLAND'S NATIONAL EMBLEM, THE TULIP

From the end of April, for eight or nine weeks, the polder between Leiden and Haarlem is transformed into a multicoloured carpet by its 8,000 hectares/20,000 acres planted with tulips. This wild flower from the steppes of central Asia, which first bloomed in Holland in 1594, aroused such a passion that growers have continued to modify its shapes and colours to this day.

Delftware tulip vase

FLOWER OF THE SULTANS

In the 16th century Ferdinand I of Austria's ambassador extraordinary to the court of the Ottoman sultan was surprised at the general passion for a flower then unknown in Europe, the tulip. He brought back a few bulbs, which were planted in the Imperial gardens in Vienna in 1554. The name *Tulp* resulted from a mistake on the ambassador's part, as 'dülbend' means turban in Persian, whereas the precious flower was called *'lale'*.

THE TAMING OF THE TULIP

A French botanist, Charles de Lécluse, who was interested in the form and structure of the tulip, discovered its fantastic capacity for hybridisation. He created the first blooms of *Tulipa gesneriana* in the Leiden botanical gardens in 1594. Little did he realise, when he made his research public, that he was unleashing a kind of madness that was to seize hold of the entire Dutch nation.

TULIPS IN ART

The tulip, precious as a silver dish or a cut-crystal glass, now became an element in the composition of still lifes. The Flemish painter Jan Breughel (1568-1625) was the first to depict it in all its ephemeral splendour. The Delft potters dedicated a special vase to the tulip, specifically designed to show off all its beauty to the greatest effect.

TULIPOMANIA

The tulip's great success as a curiosity stimulated the greed of the speculators. All kinds of people began to experiment with the aim of obtaining a flower of rare shape or colour. In 1634, the tulip was even quoted on the stock exchange and had its own lawyers to take care of transactions. The craze lasted for three years, during which time tulips were bought and sold for astronomical sums. *Semper Augustus* traded for between 4,000 and 5,500

Florins. All this speculation came to an end when the market crashed, though the tulip remained a luxury item for a very long time afterwards.

BULB CULTIVATION

The Haarlem region saw an extraordinary boom in the cultivation of bulbs, which became one of the region's main exports, due to its sandy soil, rich in limestone, which is particularly suited to growing tulips. Shortly after flowering the blooms are cut in such a way as to preserve the nutritional reserves of the bulb. These are harvested three months after the plant is cut back and go for forcing (greenhouse growing) or are stored at a variable temperature for garden planting.

HOW TO GROW YOUR TULIP

Tulip bulbs should be planted between September and early December Plant your bulbs 10 cm/4in deep, whatever type of soil you have, and

CULTIVARS

Starting from the hundred or so tulip species to be found growing wild in central Asia, horticulturalists have developed around 900 tulip varieties, or cultivars. These fall into three categories, early, mid-season or late, according to the period in the year when they flower.

leave a space twice the height of the fully-grown plants between them. Depending on their variety and size, your tulips will bloom either in March or April (for early varieties) or May (for later varieties). The earth around the bulbs should be kept damp except when there's a frost.

TOBACCO MANIA

In the 16th century a new craze hit Europe: the sniffing or smoking of the leaves of a plant discovered by Christopher Columbus among the American Indians. This luxury product, precious and rare, couldn't fail to interest the Dutch speculators, who set about acclimatising the plant in their colonies in Asia.

HERB OF THE INDIANS SMOKED AT THE ENGLISH COURT

Tobacco was cultivated intensively in Haiti by the Spanish and was at first prized for its medicinal qualities. It was sniffed to cure headaches and drunk as a decoction as a treatment for ulcers. The consumption of tobacco by smoking was a novelty introduced to the court of Elizabeth I of England by Sir Walter Raleigh, who was a great pipe-smoker.

NICOTIANA TABACUM

Although tobacco use was introduced to Holland by English soldiers, it was the merchants of the East India Company who acclimatised this American plant in Asia and South Africa. In the 18th century tobacco was regarded as a luxury and was included as a privilege in the rations given to the officers and ordinary seamen of the East India Company.

THE FAMOUS PIPES OF GOUDA

The vogue for tobacco led to the birth of a new industry manufacturing earthenware pipes. The first factories appeared in Holland around 1610, with the pipe-makers of Gouda considered the best. Each factory put its own mark on the stem of the pipe and twenty-five different marks have been identified on porcelain pipes made in Gouda.

THE TASTE OF TOBACCO

Although there are a great many varieties of tobacco, with different tastes, smells and burning qualities, it's only after two final processes, 'saucing' and 'flavouring' that they come into their own. Saucing involves flavouring the leaves with a mixture of glycerine, licorice and sugar, while in flavouring they're treated with various essences, such as rum or orange.

THE MYSTERY PIPE

Between 1900 and 1940 a new pipe, known as the mystery pipe or *'door-roker'*, was all the rage. An image would appear under the glaze as the pipe was smoked. The secret lay in the stamping of a design on the highly porous clay before the glaze was fired, which was then coloured by the nicotine.

SMOKING OR NON SMOKING?

Unlike many Anglo-Saxon countries, the Netherlands haven't adopted policies to restrict consumption of tobacco and cigarettes. In most restaurants and cafés there are

Adrian Brouwer :
Interior with tobacco smokers

> Meerschaum pipes, pipes made of wood, earthenware or porcelain, ethnic pipes from all five continents, snuffboxes, cigar, betel and opium, boxes, hookahs and opium pipes – Smokiana is a paradise for collectors of smoking paraphernalia. **Prinsengracht, 488, open Wed.-Sat. noon-6pm. ☎ 421 17 79.**

no non-smoking and smoking zones. As a result it may seem impossible to breathe when you first go into some coffee houses. However tobacco and the smell of tobacco are an important part of the atmosphere.

In the 17th century Dutch genre painters even created a new genre, that of interiors with smokers, of which Adrian Brouwer was the best exponent. In these smoky dens customers who weren't yet falling down drunk would indulge in all kinds of debauchery.

Today's coffee-shops, where tobacco isn't the only weed to be smoked, are simply perpetuating the old tradition of permissiveness and tolerance in designated places.

AMSTERDAM, CITY OF CIGARS

Amsterdam is the most important market in the world for the sale of wrappers, the leaves in which cigars are rolled, which come from Indonesia. The city is also famous for the cigars

manufactured there. Their subtle aroma is obtained by mixing fifteen to twenty different kinds of tobacco (Java, Sumatra, Havana, Brazil, and so on).

DELICIOUS DUTCH CHEESE

For many people Dutch cheese means either Edam or Gouda. Yet Holland produces many different kinds of cheese and is the top cheese-exporter in the world. It was in the Middle Ages that the Dutch began to specialise in the manufacture of pressed 'uncooked' cheese. The secret of the cheeses' taste lies in their capacity for aging and in the addition of spices from the Moluccas. Dutch cheese can be left to mature and tasted like wine, from the soft, fruity young cheeses to the spicy dryness of the older varieties.

HOW THE CHEESE IS MADE

Apart from a small amount of goat's cheese *(geitenkaas)*, most cheese in Holland is made from cow's milk. Dutch cows are among the best milk-producers in the world. Each individual animal can produce up to 6,136 litres/1,350 gallons a year. The milk is made to curdle by adding a fermenting agent and

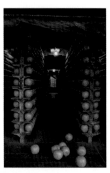

rennet. The whey is then separated from the curd by a process of stirring, and the curd is put into a mould. After it has been pressed the cheese is immersed in brine for several days. The flavour and texture of the cheese, which ages as it dries, depends on the length of time it's left to mature.

CHEESE FROM THE SOUTH...

Make sure you taste some of the delicious farm cheeses while you're in Amsterdam. They're famous for their complex flavours, which grow stronger as they age. Gouda comes in wide, flat rounds and can be eaten *jong* (three to six months old), *pittig* (eighteen months old), *oud* (two years old) or *heel oud* (two and a half years old or more). The older the cheese, the fuller the flavour. Mature Gouda tastes a bit like parmesan. It also comes in a miniature variety, called Amsterdammer, which is always eaten young.

... AND THE NORTH

Edam is the characteristic little round cheese whose deep yellow crust is covered in a layer of red wax for export.

WORDS EVERY CHEESE-LOVER SHOULD KNOW

Kaas: cheese
Boerenkaas: farm cheese made with unpasturised milk. To make sure it's the real thing, look for the special seal stamped on the crust.
Jong: young
Belegen: medium-mature
Pittig: full-flavoured
Oud: mature
Heel oud: extra-mature

It's dryer than Gouda and can be eaten at different stages: *jong*, *belegen* (one year old) and *oud* (two years old). Mimolette is another widely-exported northern cheese. Its name means 'half-soft' and comes from its consistency, which it loses as it ages.

THE GOUDA NOUVEAU HAS ARRIVED!

Gouda is made using milk flavoured with fresh herbs and, like wine, arrives in the shops at particular times of year. The soft, delicate May Gouda *(meikaas)* is around for only six weeks, from mid-June to the end of July and the Dutch celebrate its arrival, as they do that of the herring.

You can tell *Leidse kaas*, which is flavoured with cumin seeds, from Gouda by the famous crossed keys of the city of Leiden printed on its orange rind. Friesland also produces a cheese flavoured with cloves, called *Friese Nagel kaas*.

CHEESE MARKETS

The biggest cheese market is held in Alkmaar in north Holland on Friday mornings from May to October. Closer to Amsterdam

WHERE TO BUY YOUR CHEESE

If you're in Amsterdam on a Friday or Saturday, hurry along to the Amsterdamse Kaashal (Lijnbaansgracht, 32, open Fri. 9am-6pm, Sat. 9am-4pm) where you'll find the widest range of farm cheeses at very good prices. On other days, go to the market in Albert Cuypstraat or, on a Saturday, to the market in Noordermarkt. And don't forget, it's customary to taste before you buy.

(30km/20 miles) is the town of Edam itself, whose very picturesque market is held on Wednesdays in July and August 10am-12.30pm. Here the cheeses are weighed, under the eye of a bowler-hatted inspector.

DIAMONDS ARE FOREVER

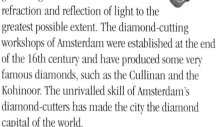

A jeweller in Antwerp cut the first faceted diamond in 1475. The full splendour of these hardest of all stones can only be seen when they're cut in a way that exploits the laws governing the refraction and reflection of light to the greatest possible extent. The diamond-cutting workshops of Amsterdam were established at the end of the 16th century and have produced some very famous diamonds, such as the Cullinan and the Kohinoor. The unrivalled skill of Amsterdam's diamond-cutters has made the city the diamond capital of the world.

THE FOUR 'C'S

Most of the diamonds cut in Amsterdam come originally from South Africa. They're bought in London, however, at the 'Sights' which take place ten times a year. Diamonds are valued according to four criteria, which are known as the four 'c's. These are the cut, colour, clarity and carat – or weight – of the stone.

FROM PYRAMID TO BRILLIANT

Diamonds are made of carbon crystallised by the combined effects of high pressures and temperatures. In their uncut state they're eight-sided. When cut in half they fall into pyramids, the shape in which they were mounted as jewels in the days before the first rose-cut was invented. The different types of cut depend on the crystal's initial shape, which may be rectangular, emerald, baguette or oblong, marquise or pear-shaped.

THE DIAMOND'S SPARKLE

The most common, but also the most expensive cut is the 'brilliant'. This

AMSTERDAM DIAMANTSTAD

consists of a 'table' surrounded by 32 upper facets, which slope at an angle of 35° towards the 24 lower facets, themselves sloping at an angle of 41°. A total of 57 facets gives the greatest possible amount of coloured sparkle, the 'fire' of the diamond.

visible presence of other elements or peculiarities of crystallisation (clouds, flaws, or feathers) takes away much of its value. Diamonds are classified into seven categories according to a scale of imperfections that are visible to the naked eye (with the aid of a magnifying glass). These range from the flawless, the purest type, to the kind with the most imperfections, known as Piqué III.

SUBTLE COLOURS

A yellowish hue is regarded as highly undesirable in a diamond. However if, as a result of the presence of another mineral in the carbon at the time of crystallisation, a diamond is tinted a uniform pink, blue, green or black, this colour gives it an enhanced value.

PURITY AND BRILLIANCE

A high-quality diamond must be completely pure. The over-

COUNTING IN CARATS

These precious jewels are weighed in metric carats, one carat being equal to two hundred milligrams/0.007oz (5 carats = 1gm/0.04oz) or a hundred points. A 0.01-carat brilliant has exactly the same number of facets as one weighing 22 carats.

COMPETITIVE PRICES

Besides giving you a greater range of size and quality, buying a diamond in a diamond-cutting shop has the added advantage of being

REAL OR FAKE?

All the diamond-cutters in Amsterdam and all the major jewellers provide certificates of authenticity. These large businesses wouldn't want to undermine their reputations by selling a zircon as a diamond. Better still, they have English-speaking sales personnel who are ready to spend the necessary time with you, presenting an entire range of diamonds to suit both your heart and your wallet.

much cheaper than at home. Prices vary from $22,000 to $3,000 per carat, depending on the quality of the stone. So a diamond cut as an emerald costs less than a brilliant for the same number of carats, since less of the substance is lost. Yellowish coloration and the presence of small inclusions are also factors that make the price of a diamond more affordable.

THE DIFFERENT SHAPES OF DIAMOND	
SQUARE PRINCESS	
BRILLIANT	
MARQUISE	
PEAR-SHAPED	
HEART-SHAPED	
PRINCESS	
OVAL	
EMERALD	
SQUARE	
BAGUETTE	

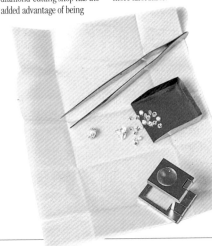

THE ART OF LIVING IN AMSTERDAM

To make up for the lack of housing in a city that has kept its organic structure almost intact since the 17th century, Amsterdammers have had to be both imaginative and practical. Pioneers of converting old buildings they invented lofts and houseboats. Another example of the city's unusual housing is the transformation of its former hospices or *hofjes*.

LOFT LIVING

Question: back in the 1970s, where could you get a room in the centre of Amsterdam at a price you could afford? Answer: on Prinseneiland and Prinsengracht, where the many abandoned workshops, disused warehouses and the odd disused church gave architects an enormous choice of spaces to convert as they chose, so long as they preserved the façade. Life without walls, abandoning the old strict separation of the different vital functions, became the challenge for those inventing a non-conformist lifestyle.

HOUSEBOATS: LIFE ON THE WATER

From old Rhine barges and rafts surmounted by little shacks, to craft that look as though they're going to sink any minute, the floating houses of Amsterdam first appeared on the city's canals in the 1950s, in response to the housing shortage. Originally inhabited by people on the fringes of society, they've become dream homes for the young and strapped for cash, since a mooring costs only 500Fl a year.

KEEPING THE NUMBERS DOWN

This type of housing, which isn't that different from squatting, was legalised in 1973 as a way of limiting the number of houseboats, which had a worrying tendency to multiply. Nowadays surveys suggest there's a fleet of 2,400 houseboats, of which only a thousand are licensed, although the others aren't illegal. They're concentrated on Prinsengracht, Brouwersgracht and the

Amstel. Of course every houseboat is connected to the telephone and the city's supplies of electricity and running water.

HOFJES

Here and there in Jordaan you'll see a sign pointing discreetly down a narrow alleyway to a *hofje*. These

former hospices, which were originally intended as housing for elderly people in need, consist of tiny houses built round a little courtyard or garden. The *hofjes* have their devotees who, with a few modifications, manage to

SOME THINGS YOU NEED TO KNOW...

Pedestrians beware! In Amsterdam the bike is king. Don't even step on to a pavement without checking whether or not it's a cycle track

If it is, a sharp 'ding-ding!' will soon remind you of the fact in no uncertain terms. And then, there's the question of punctuality. This city runs on time. Don't think you can turn up to meet someone the usual fifteen minutes late.

Hard work and simplicity are Calvinist virtues; but when the offices close at 5pm, the Dutch like to take some time to relax. After eating their evening meal between 6 and 6.30pm, they like to go on family bike rides, visit their friends or simply spend the evening in a favourite café.

create little islands of tranquillity for themselves in the bustling heart of the city.

COSY CORNER

It's hardly surprising, in a country where it's wet and windy for most of the year, that Amsterdamers' homes are places of comfort, carefully furnished and decorated and

filled with vases of flowers all year round. People here like to be comfortable and their houses tend to be fresh, tidy and impeccably clean, with that extra little something that reflects their own special decorative flair.

As soon as the sun comes out, the pavements are covered in tables and chairs. This very particular lifestyle is known as *gezelligheid*, which means at once intimate, comfortable and sociable.

'BROWN CAFÉS' AND *KRANTCAFÉS*

Cafés have always been a kind of second home to the Dutch, who don't often invite people into their own homes. The decor of the traditional 'brown cafés', or *bruine kroegen*, is all nicotine-stained walls, dark wood panelling, sparkling copper pumps and sawdust on the floor. In complete contrast, the interiors of the big cafés are generally light, spacious, and designed with a resolutely contemporary feel. These cafés tend to have a younger clientele.

KRANTCAFÉ

The Amsterdammers' favourite pastime is sitting in a café for hours on end reading the newspaper, so it would be unthinkable not to find an enormous range of daily papers *(krant)* available to the clients in your favourite café.

Some large cafés, such as the very trendy *De Jaren*, or the cosier *American Café*, even provide a large table with good lighting, where you can sit in comfort and read them all day if you so desire. English-language newspapers are sometimes available too.

THE DAILY GRIND

After the departure of the office-workers, who come in for their lunch-time snack, the afternoon hours are left to the players of cards and chess. Aperitif time starts at around 5pm, while the *eetcafés*, where a portion of the dish of the day *(dagschotel)* tends to be generous and cheap, fill up with young people, who eat all sitting round one big table.

CONVIVIAL AND CHEERY

'Brown cafés' tend to be quiet during the evening, but liven up in the evening, particularly on Friday and Saturday nights. Regulars and casual customers go there to talk in a free and easy atmosphere where social barriers come down. Most drink beer or spirits, some sing songs, others discuss the latest match or set the world to rights with friends who were strangers an hour ago.

DRINKERS' JARGON

When you order a beer you'll usually be given draught lager

brewed in Amsterdam, either Heineken or Amstel. Try asking for a 20 or 25cl *pils* (about half a pint) or, for the very thirsty, a 50cl *vaas* (about a pint). In both cases the beer should be served with a head two inches thick. The Dutch sometimes drink beer with a little chaser of *jenever* (gin).

This strange practice is known as *kopstoot,* or headbanging, no doubt because of the migraines it causes.

THE *PROEFLOKAAL*

Jenever, a spirit distilled from cereals and juniper berries, has its own places of worship, known as *proeflokalen* or tasting-houses. Here, the casks are lined up on the counter and you drink standing up, putting your lips to a little glass filled to the brim and sucking in the entire contents in one go, without losing a drop. *Jenever* is drunk either young *(jong)* or mellowed with age *(oud)* and is often served with salted herring.

ORDINARY OR DECAF?

One cup of arabica coffee contains between 50 and 100mg of caffeine and the same quantity of robusta coffee contains between 120 and 150mg, while a cup of decaffeinated coffee only contains between 1 and 2mg. Drinking large quantities of coffee

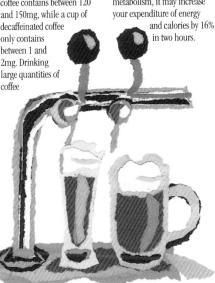

(more than nine cups a day) causes a rise in cholesterol levels of between 8 and 10%, although, as coffee acts as a stimulant and appetite suppressant, it may make you lose weight at the same time. Also, because a 100mg dose of caffeine stimulates the metabolism, it may increase your expenditure of energy and calories by 16% in two hours.

DUTCH CUISINE

It would be a bit of an exaggeration to talk about Dutch food in terms of gourmet cooking or haute cuisine. However, whilst they do not enjoy the same kind of gourmet reputation as, say, the French, quantities are usually copious. Thanks to the various immigrant communities, those with a taste for spicy food won't be disappointed and mention must be made of the *rijsttafel* combining many different Indonesian dishes and flavours.

THE SMELLS AND TASTES OF THE EAST

The first Dutch East India Company was founded in Amsterdam in 1594. This was the start of a burgeoning traffic between Holland and the Far East, particularly Indonesia, where they could buy a great quantity of spices, such as pepper, nutmeg and cloves. This long familiarity with the tastes and smells of

the East explains why Indonesian cooking has settled in so well under the grey skies of the North Sea coast.

INDONESIAN CUISINE WITH A DUTCH FLAVOUR

The travellers of times gone by were amazed at the enormous appetites of the Dutch. Their surprise is easy to understand when you sit down to eat a *rijsttafel*. This type of meal, completely unknown to the peoples of the Indonesian islands, is like some

gargantuan anthology of Indonesian flavours and consists of between eight and fifty different dishes. The Delft factories even created a specially-designed *rijsttafelstel* service, with nine different elements that fit together around a central star-shaped dish.

THE *RIJSTTAFEL*

After the prawn crackers, known as *kroepoek*, you're served with white rice *(nasi buti)* and a great variety of dishes, usually with a slightly sweet peanut sauce, which may also be rather hot and spicy. You'll have the opportunity to try steamed vegetables *(gado gado)*, marinated chicken or beef pieces cooked on skewers like kebabs (*saté*), meatballs with saffron and other dishes flavoured with coconut.

TRADITIONAL DUTCH COOKING

Simple and nourishing are the two terms which spring naturally to mind when talking about Dutch food. Whether it's the split-pea soup flavoured with ham, which has to be so thick the spoon stands upright, or *hutspot*, a meat stew with vegetables in season, you know you won't leave the table feeling hungry. If you like the sound of these specialities, and want to find out about more, turn to page 69.

turn to page 69.

HOW TO EAT A HERRING

Question: how do you eat *nieuwe haring* the way the Dutch do? Answer: tip your head back, hold your herring by its tail and dangle it into your mouth, then gulp it down in a few bites! Beware! New herrings should smell of the sea and have no dark red patches

on their backs. Wash yours down with a glass of iced *jenever*. Enjoy!

SEAFOOD

Herring fishing opens on 25 May. The Dutch are great fans of the humble herring and like to eat it raw, seasoned with peppercorns (*nieuwe haring*).

A great many *haringkar* (herring stands) are stationed along the canals all year round, serving *maatsjesharing*, or marinated herrings with onions. The eels caught in the IJsselmeer (*paling*), which may be eaten 'green' or smoked, are also a favourite with many.

Although the Dutch don't spend much time over their meals, coffee breaks are sacred. *Kopjes koffie* are drunk all day long, accompanied by something sweet, such as chocolates, delicious Droste sweets or biscuits made with spices. The greedy will find their will-power crumbles away when faced with the unbeatable fruit tart or *Limburgse vlaai*, which comes in over twenty different, mouth-watering varieties.

Amsterdam
Practicalities

GETTING AROUND

Given that Amsterdam is comparatively small and that it's very hard to get around it in a car (and even harder to find a parking space), get yourself a detailed map of the whole city at the VVV (see p. 35) and do your exploring on foot, taking your bearings from the canals. Apart from Plantage and Pijp, the districts are all arranged inside a ring of canals bordered by the Singelgracht. You should allow two days to explore the main attractions of Amsterdam, assuming you take a tram or boat every now and then to get you from one district to another. If the weather's good, the most pleasant way to get around quickly is by bicycle and you can rent one very cheaply. If you do, you'll really be doing as the Amsterdammers do.

BY METRO, TRAM AND BUS

These run from 6am to midnight. After that, there's a night bus service.

The public transport network covers a wide area, and is quick, cheap and easy to use. There are 3 metro lines, 17 tram routes, 5 bus routes and 8 night bus routes covering the city centre and suburbs.

Most of the trams leaving from the central station pass through the Dam and Muntplein. For other stops, consult your map or ask the driver, who'll give you the information you need in English. The metro won't be much use to you unless you're going to east Amsterdam. If you've hired a bike, though, remember there's nothing to stop you taking it on the metro with you.

Single tickets (3Fl) can be bought in the metro and from bus and tram drivers, but it's better value to buy a pass in advance. You can buy one lasting 24 hours (12Fl) or 2, 3 or 4 days, or you can buy a *strippenkaart* with 15 or 45 boxes that you have validated by the driver or by machine (you use two boxes per journey within the centre zone). Once validated, it allows you to travel on different forms of transport for a period of 1 hour. The cards are on sale in the GVB kiosk opposite the central station and in newsagents' or tobacco shops or from automatic ticket dispensers in the rail and metro stations. To get on or off the tram or metro, press the button marked '*deur open*'.

BY BIKE

Bikes have a great many advantages: no parking problems, no hills, absolute priority over cars and pedestrians (who are given a mouthful if they dare set so

much as a toe on the sacrosanct cycle lanes) and no worries about timetables. The only disadvantage is that you might find your vehicle has been stolen, as happens fairly often. So when hiring your bike, make sure it comes with a good lock. Rental gets cheaper the more days you take. Remember, though, that most of these bikes have only one gear and that you put the brakes on by pedalling backwards, which can take some getting used to. Bike hire offices are open seven days a week from 9am to 6pm.

When you hire a bike, you'll be asked for proof of identity and a deposit of 50Fl or your credit card details.

Koenders Take a bike
☎ 624 83 91.
You'll find the cheapest daily and weekly rates near the central station.

Mac Bike ☎ 626 69 64.
Marnixstraat, 220.
Rents out solid Dutch bikes at good rates.

Bike city ☎ 626 37 21.
Bloemgracht, 68-70. This shop will provide you with route suggestions and two anti-theft devices.

Yellow Bike ☎ 620 69 40.
Nieuwezijds Kolk, 29.
Guided cycle tours through Amsterdam or the nearby countryside, conducted in English. Make sure you reserve in advance.

BY PEDALO

You can hire a *canalbike* or two or four-seater pedalo at the following piers: near Leidseplein, between the Rijksmuseum and the Heineken brewery, opposite the Westerkerk and on Keizersgracht/Leidsestraat. There's a 50Fl deposit. You'll be given a map of the canals and ideas for routes. You can return your pedalo to any pier you choose. Open April to October from 10am to 10pm, and November to March from 10am to 5.30pm (10.30pm in summer).
☎ 626 55 74.

BY BOAT

Travel by *canalbus* is fun and very pleasant in summer. A shuttle service runs every 20 mins between the central station and the Rijksmuseum from 10am to 8pm. There's a fixed charge of 17.50Fl for the day, which allows you to get on or off whenever and wherever you like. The canalbuses stop at Leidseplein, at the intersection of Leidsestraat and Keizersgracht, and at Anne Frank's house on Prinsengracht. The whole journey takes about an hour. Tickets can be bought in hotels and Canalbus kiosks. Two-hour candlelit trips with wine and gouda tasting run on Friday and Saturday evenings, leaving from the Rijksmuseum at 9.30pm (☎ 623 98 86).

BY TAXI

There aren't many taxis in the city and they're expensive, so Amsterdammers tend to use them most frequently for journeys at night. You'll find taxi ranks outside the central station, on the Dam, Leidseplein, Rembrandtplein, Nieuwmarkt, Waterlooplein and Spui. The central telephone number is
☎ 677 77 77.

Although the classic taxi is little used in the city centre, you can get to your hotel quickly by watertaxi. Many hotels have special landing stages for just this reason. Watertaxis have a standard meter (about 2Fl a minute) and a radio telephone. The most luxurious of them can carry as many as 8 people
☎ 622 21 81.

The service run by the museum boat (*museumboot*) takes you on a complete tour of the city, starting from the central station and travelling along the loveliest canals before returning to its point of departure via the port. Guided tours with a commentary leave every 30 mins (45 mins in winter) from 10am to 5pm, making six stops, enabling you to visit a museum or do some shopping. You can buy a ticket for the whole day (22Fl) or half a day (15Fl) from the VVV or at the Rederij Lovers kiosk opposite the central station (☎ 622 21 81). This will also get you a 10 to 50% reduction on your museum entrance fee.

If you like the idea of a one-hour sight-seeing trip on a river boat, by day or night, there are a number of organisations running these every 15 mins from 6 to 10pm. You can leave from either the central station or the Rokin.

Last but not least, absolutely the best way to tour the canals in real style is to hire an elegant wooden saloon boat dating from 1920. The captain will see to your every need, you'll have access to the bar and you can even order a buffet if you so choose.

This magnificent saloon boat holds a maximum of 12 people (Salonboot *'Paradis'* ☎ 684 93 38).

USING THE TELEPHONE

To phone outside Holland, dial 00 followed by the number for the country you're calling, then the specific number you want to call.

If you're calling Amsterdam from another town in the Netherlands, dial 020 before the seven digit number.

Public telephone boxes are green, as is the logo of the post office and telephone company. Public phones take coins (25c, 1, 2.5 and 5Fl) or magnetic cards costing 5, 10 or 25Fl, which you can buy in post offices and newsagents' shops. Most will also accept international credit cards. If you make your call from the Telecenter (Raadhuistraat, 48), which is open day and night, you can pay for it either in cash or with a credit card or traveller's cheques. It's cheaper to call after 6.30pm or at the weekend. Lastly, if you use the telephone in your hotel room, remember you'll be fairly heavily surcharged.

Dialling codes from the Netherlands:

UK ☎ 00 44

Ireland ☎ 00 353

USA and Canada ☎ 00 1

Australia ☎ 00 61

New Zealand ☎ 00 64

For internal direct enquires call ☎ 06 8008 and for international enquiries call ☎ 06 0418.

You can buy stamps at any post office, open from 9am to 6pm on weekdays and until 1pm on Saturdays. or simply buy them together with your postcards from a tobacconist's or souvenir shop. Post letters going outside Holland in the slot marked *'overige postcodes'* in the red letterboxes (mailboxes).

No mercy for car drivers

The fact that you've got a foreign number plate won't mean a thing! If you've forgotten to pay for your parking space (4.25Fl/hour from 9am-7pm except Sundays), you'll be disagreeably surprised to find your car immobilised by a clamp. It will cost you 130Fl to get it removed. So leave your car in a car park or buy an all-day parking permit (13.50-25.50Fl, depending on the district you're in).

To have a clamp removed or to buy a parking permit:
Dienst Stadstoezcht, Bakkerstraat, 13 (Rembrandtsplein) ☎ 639 24 69 ; Cruquiuskade, 25 ☎ 553 01 21 or **Stadstoezicht** ☎ 553 03 33.

BUREAUX DE CHANGE

Banks are open from 9 or 10am to 5 or 6pm Tuesday to Friday and

from 1pm on Mondays.

At the weekend, it will be best to change your money and traveller's cheques in the GWK branches at Schiphol airport and the Centraal Station, which are

open 24 hours. The other bureaux de change, which you'll find open on every street corner, charge a commission of between 10 and 15Fl per transaction. Many cash machines allow you to withdraw money directly using a credit or debit card. Although commission is charged, it's at an advantageous rate similar to that of traveller's cheques. A word of warning, though: withdraw a large amount each time because you pay commission on every withdrawal you make. If you have an American Express card, go straight to the American Express office, where you can withdraw money without paying any commission at all (Damrak, 66 ☎ 520 77 77). Non-members pay between 5Fl and 7.5Fl per transaction without further commission.

Avoid changing money at your hotel, where the rates will be appalling.

TOURIST INFORMATION VVV

Stationplein, 10; Leidseplein, 12; Schiphol Plaza (airport) ☎ 06 340 340 66.

As well as information leaflets and maps of Amsterdam and the surrounding area, you'll find English-speaking staff, who will be able to provide details of coming events, excursions and hotels and make bookings for you if required. The tourist information office also has a bureau de change (no commission but a slightly lower rate). The office at the central station is always extremely busy (open daily 8am-8pm), so it's better to visit the one located in a kiosk opposite (daily 9am-5pm) or the one on Leidseplein (daily 8am-7pm).

MUSEUM OPENING TIMES

Most of the museums are open from 10am to 5pm on weekdays and from 1pm on Sundays. Some are closed on Mondays. The large museums (Rijksmuseum, Van Gogh and Stedelijk) are open every day from 10am to 5pm. On state holidays, they follow the Sunday opening times, except for 1 January, 25 December and 30 April, when they're closed all day.

On presentation of a valid ID card there are reduced rates for students and senior citizens (over 65), plus there are reductions for under 18s. 'Museum Cards' are available in VVV and NBT offices and participating museums – valid for a year, they give free admission to all the main museums, but for a price.

USEFUL ADDRESSES

Centrale Medical Service
☎ 06 350 320 42

Police
Main station, Elandsgracht, 117
☎ 559 91 11;
Lijnbaansgracht, 219;
Nieuwezijds Voorburgwal, 104;
Prinsengracht, 1109.

Emergencies
☎ 112

Lost property
Schiphol airport ☎ 649 14 33;
Trains ☎ 557 85 44;
Trams, bus, métro ☎ 551 44 08.

The Béguinage:
a real sense of the past

A stone's throw from the bustle of Kalverstraat, the Béguinage is an island of calm on Spui square, an elegant, triangular space where history and culture meet. Also here you'll find the city's favourite 'brown café', two trendy cafés, one opposite the other, and a great bookshop. The Béguinage is thought to have taken its name from a Flemish preacher, Lambert Le Bègue, who was influential in Flanders.

❶ Spui ★

Once home to the *Provos,* who used to dance madly round the statue of 't Lievertje, a kind of Amsterdam street urchin symbolising their rebellious spirit. The square has since been restored and is now the cultural heart of Amsterdam. A market for old books is held there every Friday and one for contemporary art every Sunday.

❷ The Béguinage
(Begijnhof) ★★★
Entrance on Spui indicated by a carved sign.
Free entry.

A narrow, vaulted passageway leads to this charming garden surrounded by 17th and 18th-century houses. The devout,

celibate Béguine nuns have been replaced by old ladies or women students of slender means. In the centre of the lawn stands a medieval church, while number 34 is the city's oldest house, built of wood and dating from 1477.

❸ Gallery of the civil guard★ (Schuttersgalerij)

Same opening hours as the historical museum.Entry free.

This covered passage between the historical museum and Béguine convent houses huge portraits of the civil guard who were charged with

protecting one the eleven districts in the city.

❹ Amsterdam Historical Museum★★
(Amsterdams Historisch Museum)
Kalverstraat, 92, Nieuwezijds Voorburgwal, 357
☎ 523 18 22
Open Mon.-Fri. 10am-5pm, Sat. and Sun. 11am-5pm. Entry charge.

History unfolds step by step in this very informative museum housed in a former orphanage for boys and girls, built in the 15th century and extended in the 17th. Everyday life in Amsterdam since the 13th century is evoked through art, maps and models.

❺ Café Hoppe★★
Spui, 18-20
☎ 420 44 20.

A real Amsterdam institution since 1670, frequented by both locals and passing customers. The narrow, wood-panelled space with sawdust on the floor is always thick with smoke and packed to bursting point, overflowing on to the square in good weather.

❻ Lucius★★
(fish restaurant) Spuistraat, 247
☎ 624 18 31
Open every day except Sun. 5-11pm.

No two ways about it, this is the best fish restaurant in town, simply decorated with pottery and rustic tables and the dishes of the day chalked up on a blackboard. Here you can eat fish and seafood specialities subject to availability, served without fuss, and with a great choice of liqueurs and spirits to round off your meal.

❼ VRANKRIJK SQUAT ★
Spuistraat, 214-216.

Squatting has gone out of style. All the same, a few of the indomitable old guard have bought their squat and turned the former home of the *Handelsblad* daily newspaper into a sort of monument-cum-memorial to the huge 'Provo' protest movement, which was strong in the 1970s. Today the grunge evenings, badges and graffiti in loud colours and 'kill the pigs' on the façade are just a pale reflection of the way it used to be.

❽ Atheneum Boekhandel★

Spui, 14-16
☎ 622 62 48
Mon. 11am-6pm, Tue.-Sat. 9.30am-6pm, Sun. noon-5.30pm, Thu. until 9pm.

Like the square, this lovely bookshop, with its Art Nouveau-style decor, is very elegant and very busy. Try the main shop for the latest best-seller or a CD. If you're looking for a foreign language newspaper, go to the annexe next door.

The Dam: heart of the city

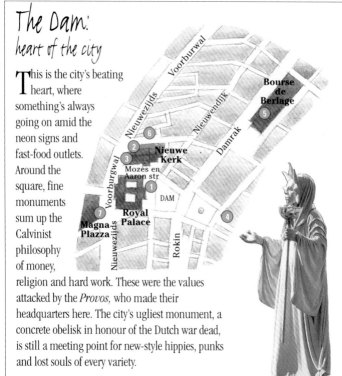

This is the city's beating heart, where something's always going on amid the neon signs and fast-food outlets. Around the square, fine monuments sum up the Calvinist philosophy of money, religion and hard work. These were the values attacked by the *Provos,* who made their headquarters here. The city's ugliest monument, a concrete obelisk in honour of the Dutch war dead, is still a meeting point for new-style hippies, punks and lost souls of every variety.

❶ Royal Palace★ (*Koninklijk Paleis*)
Dam

Open every day Jun.-Jul. 10am-6pm, Aug. noon-5.30pm, Sep.-May 1-4pm Entry charge.

Before becoming Louis Bonaparte's royal residence, this inelegant, austere building was the town hall, designed by the famous 17th-century architect Jacob van Campen. Don't miss the superb tiled floor in the Burghers' Hall (*Burgerzaal*) showing maps of the northern and southern hemispheres. Today the queen comes here only for official receptions.

❷ New Church★★ (*Nieuwe Kerk*)
Dam
☎ 638 69 09
Open every day during temporary exhibitions 10am-5pm. Entry charge.

This church was built in the Flamboyant Gothic style and modified many times over the years. Today it houses exhibitions and concerts. Its stained glass, bronze chandeliers, mahogany pulpit (1649) and superb choir stalls are perfectly set off by the very sparse, Calvinist interior. All the kings and queens of the Netherlands have been crowned here in accordance with tradition.

❸ Palette★
Nieuwezijds Voorburgwal, 125
☎ 639 32 07
Mon.-Wed. 1-6pm, Tue., Thu. and Fri. 11am-6pm, Sat. 11am-5pm.

Leaning up against the New Church is the city's smallest shop, specialising in making silk and satin shoes. With a choice of over 500 colours, there's no way you could fail to find just the right shoes and accessories to go with your little evening dress.

❹ Hotel Krasnapolsky★
Dam, 9
☎ 554 91 11

Make sure you have your lunch, or even just a cup of tea, in this 19th-century palace. An immense, amazing winter garden recalls the magnificence of the Belle Époque. The decor in the restaurant consists of black and white floor tiles, frescoes on the walls and large palms, and, to cap it all, the food is excellent too (buffet lunch and breakfast).

❺ Beurs van Berlage ★★★
Damrak, 277
☎ 550 41 13
Museum open Tue.-Sun. 10am-4pm.

This imposing building along Damrak, has a red-brick façade 141m/463ft long designed by H.P. Berlage. In 1903 its sober, functional shapes represented a complete

break with the past. There's a fine view of the city from the top of its 39m/128ft tower if you can climb the 95 very steep steps. The large hall with its perfect acoustics, home of the Netherlands Philharmonic Orchestra, stages concerts all year round.

❻ De Drie Fleschjes★★
Gravenstraat, 18
☎ 624 84 43
Open Mon.-Sat. noon-8.30pm, Sun. 3-8pm.

The city's finest *proeflokaal* was founded by the Bootz distillery in 1650. Journalists and stockbrokers congregate here at the end of the day, hanging their jackets on the taps of the barrels before drinking a few *borrels* of *jenever*. Also on show here is a unique collection of portraits of the mayors of Amsterdam, all painted on little bottles.

❼ Magna Plazza★
Nieuwezijds Voorburgwal, 182
☎ 626 91 99
Mon. 11am-7pm, Tue.-Wed., Fri.-Sat. 10am-7pm, Sun. noon-6pm, Thu. 9am-9pm.

Cornelis Peters, the architect of this pretentious neo-Gothic construction in brick and white stone, received more than a few sarcastic comments back in 1899. Originally the central post office, it has since been transformed into an elegant shopping centre. The stairwell is worth seeing.

Rokin: for a saturday afternoon stroll

Map labels: Kalver, Oude Turfmarkt, Allard Pierson Museum, Staal Straat, Straat, Rokin, Nieuwe Doelenstraat, Heiligenweg, Amstel, De Bonneterie, MUNT PLEIN, Singel, Bloemen Markt

This was once a favourite haunt of Amsterdam's bourgeoisie, who would promenade up and down along the side of the inner dock *(rak-in)* past the most prestigious establishments in the city. For this was home to the large banks, the best diamond merchants, the most prominent antique dealers and Hajenius, cigar-makers since 1826, all of which could boast that their clientele included royalty. Today the dock has been filled in to make way for cars and trams and the prestige businesses find themselves sharing their space with other, less exclusive shops.

❶ Mint Tower★ *(Munttoren)*
Muntplein, 12.

In 1620 Hendrick de Keyser

used the remains of an old city gate as a base on which to build a Baroque wooden bell tower. Nowadays the chimes ring out every quarter of an hour. The tiny shop on the ground floor sells authentic Delft and Makkum ware, both modern and period, and is well worth visiting.

❷ Flower market ★★ *(Bloemenmarkt)*
Singel
Mon.-Sat. 8am-5.30pm, also Sun. 9am-5pm in summer.

The flower-sellers' barges are permanently moored to the banks of the Singel, to form a brightly-coloured floating market. It's always a pleasure to wander past the stalls covered in bouquets of cut and dried flowers, displaying valuable bonsais, or simply piled high with a variety of bulbs.

❸ Café De Jaren★
Nieuwedoelenstraat, 20-22
☎ 625 57 71
Open every day 10am-1am (2am Fri-Sat).

This trendiest of the large cafés, by the side of the Amstel and designed by Onno de Vries, is wonderfully light and spacious. In fine weather it's hard to find a free table on the wide floating terrace. A favourite haunt of students and businessmen alike, who come here for a late breakfast or quick lunch.

4 Staalstraat★★

This charming street straddles two canals by means of drawbridges. It's home to a great many shops, including the art bookshop Nijhot & Lee and Puccini the confectioner's. The lovely gabled house at number 7b is the former drapers' hall, headquarters of the drapers' guild whose portraits were painted by Rembrandt (*Drapers Syndic*, Rijksmuseum, see p. 60).

5 Allard Pierson Museum★★
Oude Turfmarkt, 127
☎ 525 25 56
Open Tue.-Fri. 10am-5pm, Sat., Sun. and bank holidays 1-5pm. Entry charge.

This pint-sized and highly educational archeological museum is perfect for learning about the daily life of the Mediterranean peoples of antiquity through objects and models. You can write your name in hieroglyphs on a computer or admire beautiful Parthian and Sassanid jewellery.

6 La Maison De Bonneterie★
Rokin, 140
☎ 626 21 62
Open Mon.1-5.30pm, Tue.-Sat. 10am-5.30pm late opening Thu., Sun. noon-5pm.

This is a real old-fashioned department store, boasting the title of 'Supplier to the Queen', which still has three floors where you can buy timeless and hard-wearing English clothes for the whole family, or an entire set of golfing accessories. Similarly quaint is the Grand Café on the first floor, where respectable old ladies come to take their afternoon tea.

7 P.G.C. Hajenius★★
Rokin, 92-96
☎ 623 74 94
Mon. noon-6pm, Tue.-Sat. 9.30am-6pm, Thu. until 9pm, Sun. noon-5pm.

8 ANDRIES DE JONG *SHIP SHOP*★
Muntplein, 8
☎ 624 52 51.

If you've always dreamed of turning your flat into a pleasure-cruiser, look no further. This is the shop for you, with barometers, storm-lamps, cabin lamps, pirate flags and compasses – in other words every conceivable gadget for people with a passion for sailing, whether in dreams or reality.

An Amsterdam institution. The prestigious Hajenius cigar-maker's, with its decor of dark wood, marble, lamps and accessories in pure Art Deco style, has been making subtly-blended, aromatic cigars for 170 years.

From Nieuwmarkt to Prinsenhof: the real Amsterdam

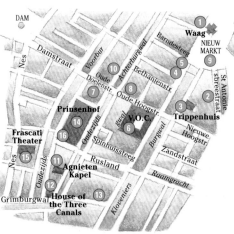

The shady canals are lined with traditional shops and former convents, now converted into cafés, giving this picturesque university quarter its special character. Here you'll find experimental theatres and secondhand book stalls, cannabis-smokers and herring-eaters. This is village Amsterdam, where everybody knows everybody else.

❶ Waag★
Nieuwmarkt.

In the 17th century the massive tower of the St Anthony Gate, a rare remnant of the medieval city wall, housed the public weighing station *(waag)*. The hall on the upper floor, formerly occupied by the Surgeons' Guild was where Rembrandt painted his first famous picture: *The Anatomy Lesson of Professor Tulp.*

❷ Nieuwmarkt metro station★
When the houses in this district were due for demolition to make way for the building of the metro, the people then squatting in them were rather brutally dislodged. So it's a little surprising to find they're the subjects of a photo exhibition in the metro station, which records the violent confrontations between squatters and police during the evictions of 1975.

❸ Trippenhuis★★
Kloveniersburgwal, 29.

This imposing old building built in the Renaissance style in 1660 is one of the few in Amsterdam that can compete with the palaces of Venice. Its owners, the Trip brothers, made their fortunes from the arms trade. Across the canal at no. 26, you can see the much smaller house which was home to their coachman.

4 Jacob Hooy & Co. herbalists★
Kloveniersburgwal, 10-12
☎ 624 30 41
Mon. noon-6pm, Tue.-Fri. 8am-6pm, Sat. 8am-5pm.

For a hundred and fifty years members of the same Oldeboom family have stood behind the counter in this deliciously spicy-smelling shop. The wooden casks that line the shelves and the polished drawers contain no fewer than six hundred different kinds of aromatic plants. The delicious licorice sweets are not to be missed.

5 Café Maximiliaan★★
Kloveniersburgwal, 6-8
☎ 626 62 80.

This café-brasserie has been opened on the site of the former Bethany convent. It specialises in strong, amber beers, which are brewed in huge copper vats in a room at the back. They also sell wonderful food here, made from recipes that include beer as an ingredient.

6 The VOC building★★
Oude Hoogstraat, 24.

In the 17th and 18th centuries this large building in red brick and yellow stone, bearing the monogram of the *Vereenige Oostindische Compagnie*, was the headquarters of the very famous Dutch East India Company, which brought back spices, coloured fabrics and porcelain from the East. Public sales of these goods were held twice yearly in the courtyard.

7 't Haringhuis Jan Hendriks★★
Oude Doelenstraat, 18
☎ 622 12 84
Open Tue.-Sat. 9am-6pm.

Whatever time it is, take a few minutes to stop off at Amsterdam's finest fishmonger's.

Jan Hendriks and his wife will let you into all the subtle secrets of the herrings you can sample in the room at the back with a little glass of *korenwijn*. You'll even get this for nothing if you go during the week after 28 May, when the herring fishing season opens.

8 Capsicum★★
Oude Hoogstraat, 1
☎ 623 10 16
Open Mon. 1-6pm,
Tue.-Sat. 10am-6pm,
Thu. until 9pm.

The sparkling colours encourage you to set off on your travels, while classical music plays gently in the background. This very classy shop sells fabrics for upholstery and dress-making. You'll find linens, cottons and silks, mostly from India and Thailand, including the shop's speciality of wonderful embroidered silks. If these aren't what you're looking for, you can also buy batik fabrics here, as well as their more everyday cousins, muslin and cotton tie-dye scarves.

9 NIEUWMARKT SQUARE

The city council called on two Dutch sculptors, Alexander Schabracq and Tom Postma, to revamp Nieuwmarkt. These two, who also worked on Damrak, are responsible for the lampposts and green railings inspired by Russian Constructivism. Not everybody likes these new additions, but at least they don't get in anyone's way.

10 Museum of Marijuana★
Oudezijds Achterburgwal, 148
☎ 623 59 61
Open every day 11am-10pm
Entry charge.

If you want to know more about marijuana and the various uses it can be put to, come to this museum, the only one of its kind in Europe, retracing ten thousand years of the history of the cannabis plant. You'll discover how, before being grown in people's cellars and sold in smokable form in coffee-shops, it was used extensively in the port of Amsterdam... but only in the manufacture of hemp ropes.

11 Chapel of St Agnes★
(Agnietenkapel)

Oudezijds Voorburgwal, 231
☎ 525 33 39
University museum open
Mon.-Fri. 9am-5pm
Entry charge.

Apart from the chapel, built in 1397, all the buildings belonging to the former medieval convent of the Agnites were given the new name of *Illustrae Atheneum*, the city's first university, in 1632. On the first floor you can see the oldest teaching room in Amsterdam, a lecture theatre with a beautiful painted ceiling decorated with Renaissance motifs, which is still in use today.

into the royal palace. In 1966, the marriage of Queen Beatrix was celebrated in the Art Deco wedding hall.

⓯ Frascati theater★
Nes, 63
☎ **626 68 66.**

In this long, narrow road you'll find a small experimental theatre specialising in plays and choreography of a resolutely

⓬ House of the three canals★★
Intersection of Oudezijds Voorburgwal, Oudezijds Achterburgwal and Grimburgwal canals.

This fine old building from the 17th-century golden age, with its distinctive red shutters and two-tone façade, was built at the point where three canals meet and was the last building to the south-east of the medieval city. Today it's home to a publishing house.

⓭ Passage Oude Manhuispoort★
Book fair Mon.-Sat. 1-4pm.

The secondhand booksellers have made their home in the niches of a covered passageway that links two canals, the Oudezijds Achterburgwal and the Kloveniersburgwal. Have a look at the lovely inner courtyard of the University of Amsterdam and the old engravings which will transport you back to the Amsterdam of the past.

⓮ Prinsenhof★★★ (The Grand hotel)
Oudezijds Voorburgwal, 197
☎ **555 31 11.**

In the 16th century this luxury hotel was the residence of princes. It's still called the 'Court of Princes' despite the fact that it was the town hall until 1986, after the town hall on the Dam was transformed

contemporary kind . You don't always have to understand Dutch to watch one of these sometimes unnerving shows. The café next door, which serves light meals until midnight, is frequented mainly by theatrical types.

⓰ Café Roux★
Oudezijds Voorburgwal, 197
☎ **555 31 11**
Open every day.

This Art Deco brasserie used to be the place where the town hall employees had their lunch and is now one of the best addresses in Amsterdam if you like French regional cooking or just want to have a cup of tea. It also houses a fresco by a member of the Cobra art movement, which, the title tells you, depicts children asking questions (1949).

The red light district: where anything goes

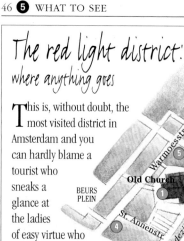

T his is, without doubt, the most visited district in Amsterdam and you can hardly blame a tourist who sneaks a glance at the ladies of easy virtue who sit in their windows all cosy and warm, waiting for clients. The district is fairly quiet during the day, but livens up in the evening when the neon signs light up. The curious public crowds along the quaysides, accosted by pimps and dealers and beguiled by the oriental scents wafting towards them from Zeedijk and the very discreet Chinatown of Amsterdam. The biggest irony is that this rather unholy district also contains two churches, one of which is hidden.

❶ Old Church★★
(Oude Kerk)
Oude Kerksplein, 23
☎ 625 82 84
Sun. 4-5pm, bell-ringing concert.

This church, with little houses clinging to its sides, looks like an abandoned ship in the middle of an ocean of sin. Its buildings, especially the Gothico-Renaissance-style octagonal bell-tower, used to be used by sailors to get their bearings. It fell victim to the iconoclastic fury of the Calvinists in the late 16th century, and this explains the sparseness of its interior, which is occasionally used for concerts.

❷ Amstelkring Museum★★★
Oudezijds Voorburgwal, 40
☎ 624 66 04
Open Mon.-Sat. 10am-5pm, Sun. 1-5pm
Entry charge.

The attic of this pretty bourgeois house conceals a secret Catholic chapel which was set up in 1663, when Catholics lost their right to worship in their own way. The house itself is also worth a visit for its heavy Dutch furniture, its tablecloths, its two kitchens with their Delft tiles and its many nooks and crannies.

❸ Oudezijds Voorburgwal★
It was probably inevitable that this canal, a stone's throw from the old port, would become the headquarters of

the city's sinners. The word 'sex' leaps out in bold or neon letters from almost every shop front, vital information just in case you're not quite sure what trade is being plied by the scantily-clad ladies in the windows.

❹ Condomerie Het Gulden Vlies★
Warmoesstraat, 141
☎ 627 41 74
Open Mon.-Sat. 11am-6pm.

The years of AIDS have given a new boost to condoms. They now come in a range of tastes and colours and some very improbable shapes, such as cow's udders, hands, Mickey mouses and dummies. Plenty of amusing gift ideas.

❺ Geels & Co★★
Warmoesstraat, 67
☎ 624 06 83
Open Mon.-Sat.
9.30am-6pm.

No, this isn't a coffee-shop, it's a shop where excellent coffee, ground on the premises, has been sold for the last hundred

and fifty years. The owners will be only too pleased to show you their collection of grinding machines and mills upstairs.

❻ The Greenhouse Effect
Warmoesstraat, 53
☎ 623 74 62.

Make sure you have a drink in this renowned coffee-shop, where you can absorb the extraordinary atmosphere of these establishments that have no equivalent anywhere else in Europe. Consult the menu above the counter to get an idea of the wares on offer.

❼ Cirelli restaurant★★
Oudezijdskolk, 69
☎ 624 35 12
Open every day after 6pm, booking advisable.

This former warehouse, renovated with a touch of fantasy, is the place to eat the best pasta in town. Make sure you take a good look at the central table sculpture by sculptor Alexander Schabracq. And don't forget to notice the lamps either.

❽ The Tower of Weeping Women★ *(Schreierstoren)*
Prins Hendrikkade, 94
☎ 624 80 52.

It is said that from this tower sailors' wives used to watch their menfolk as they sailed away, possibly never to return. It's now home to a café (1st floor) and shop (2nd floor) selling almanacs, sky charts and the very valuable *Bolle* barometers.

> *Like voluptuous figures by Rubens, they sit in state in their armchairs, next to a vase of paper roses, in the intimacy of the lamplight. In Amsterdam, vice itself takes on an old-fashioned air of warm good humour and contemplation.*
>
> Klaus Mann, 1952

The old Jewish quarter: a thriving district

Cross over the Amstel and you enter a ghost town dominated by the highly controversial mass of the Stopera. The building of the metro and the drive towards better housing have finished the destructive job begun by the Second World War. Jewish people still gather here on Saturdays for services in the large synagogue but, apart from that, the flea market on Waterlooplein is the only thing that brings a little life to the area.

❶ Portuguese Synagogue★★★
(*Esnoga*)
Mr Visserplein, 3
☎ 624 53 51
Open Sun.-Fri. 10am-4pm.
Entry charge.

This enormous brick cube with its huge windows is really a synagogue, and one of the most beautiful in Europe. It's financed by the community of 'Portuguese' Jews, descended from people who were driven out of Portugal by the Spanish Inquisition and, miraculously, still looks just the way it did when it was first opened back in 1675.

❷ Rembrandt's house★★ (*Rembrandthuis*)
Jodenbreestraat, 4-6
☎ 638 46 68
Open Mon.-Sat. 10am-5pm.
Sun. 1-5pm. Entry charge.

Rembrandt bought this superb Renaissance house in 1639 with his wife Saskia's dowry. He lived here for 20 years, painting his finest pictures in his first-floor studio. But a different aspect of the artist's formidable talent is on show here in a display of 250 engravings arranged by theme, including genre scenes, self portraits, nudes and landscapes.

❸ Pintohuis★
Sint Antoniebreestraat, 69
☎ 624 31 84.

In 1651 Isaac Pinto, a rich Jewish banker, spent the tidy sum of 35,000 florins building himself this lovely Italianate

palace, which certainly comes as a surprise in this much altered district. Indeed it almost disappeared as a result of a road-building project.

❹ Waterloopleinmarkt ★★
Waterlooplein
Mon.-Sat. 10am-5pm.

This is the Rommelmarkt (translate as flea market), the market most frequented by Amsterdammers themselves. With legal and illegal objects, army surplus and house clearances, this is the land of junk merchants and wheeler-

dealers. You might also find the Dutch bicycle of your dreams or an old cradle you can restore.

❺ Museum of Jewish history★ *(Joods Historisch Museum)*
Jonas Daniel Meijerplein, 2-4
☎ 626 99 45
Open every day 11am-5pm
Entry charge.

This museum is housed in four synagogues of the Ashkenazi community, linked by glass-covered walkways. Objects, photos and documents are arranged by theme to illustrate the life and culture of the Jews who have lived in Amsterdam since the late 16th century.

❻ Muziektheaﾠ Stopera★★
Waterlooplein, 22/Aﾠ
☎ 551 89 11/551 9ﾠ

The enormous modeﾠ complex that dominaﾠ Amstel houses the neﾠ hall and an opera hoﾠ with seats for 1,600. The building's highly controversial aesthetics and the extra destruction it necessitated in a district that had already been blighted

❽ AMSTEL DIAMOND LIMITED★
Amstel, 206-208
☎ 623 14 79
Open Mon.-Sat. 9am-5pm, Sun. 10am-5pm.

Although the Jews were forbidden to do many kinds of work by the city council, they had a monopoly of the cutting and sale of diamonds and excelled at this trade as a result. In this small, family-owned cutting shop you can see all the stages in the transformation of the uncut stone into a brilliant.

by the planners generated some violent reactions. It opened in 1986 and is still known as the Stopera, the name given to it by its critics. It does have remarkable acoustics, however.

❼ Blue bridge★ *(Blauwbrug)*
Built for the universal exhibition of 1883, this bridge crosses the majestic Amstel. It was this river which gave rise to the city itself, as well as its name of 'Amstel-dam'.

Jordaan: from cafés to culture

This is the district Amsterdammers themselves like best. With its tight network of little streets and houses, its nicotine-stained 'brown cafés', little courtyards full of flowers, tiny shops, barge-filled canals and bird market, it's here that the soul and irreverent humour of Amsterdam's ordinary people are preserved intact. It was built outside the city in the 17th century, to house the class of labourers and craftsmen, with Prinsengracht as its natural border with the world of the wily bourgeoisie. Although somewhat gentrified these days, it retains its own language and folklore, which come intensely alive during the Jordaan festival in September.

❶ Western Church★★ (Westerkerk)

Westerplein
Bell tower open Apr.-Sep. Mon.-Sat. 10am-4pm, bell-ringing concert noon-1pm
Entry charge.

Regarded as Hendrick de Keyser's masterpiece, this was the first Renaissance-style church to be built after the Reform. At the top of the 85m/279ft bell tower you can see the imperial crown, added to the city's coat of

arms by Emperor Maximilian of Austria.

❷ Coppenhagen, 1001 kralen★
Rozengracht, 54
☎ 624 36 81
Open Mon. 1-6pm, Tue.-Fri. 10am-6pm, Sat. 10am-5pm.

On the shelves you'll see hundreds of jars filled with gleaming glass beads of every conceivable colour, with antique beads from Murano and Bohemia, which were once used as items of exchange in trade with African princes, and more recently-made beads from India, Indonesia, Germany and Venice.

❸ Anne Frank house★
Prinsengracht, 263
☎ 556 71 00
Open every day 9am-5pm and Apr.-Aug. 9am-9pm Entry charge.

If you're not put off by the long queues, you can visit the *achterhuis, or* 'house behind', where the teenage Anne Frank lived like a hermit with her family, eight people in all, for two years before being deported and dying in the Belsen concentration camp. Her personal diary gives a poignant account of this time. Since it was found it has been published in almost fifty different languages. The money from sales of the book is partly used to fund the Anne Frank Foundation, which combats racism.

❹ Bloemgracht★

In the 17th century this canal, the canal of flowers, was inhabited by cloth-dyers. Today it's one of the smartest canals in Jordaan, lined with beautiful gabled houses bearing coats of arms identifying the trades of the occupants. Three of these, numbers 87, 89 and 91 have typical façades.

❺ Sint Andrieshofje★★
Egelantiersgracht, 107
Free entry.

Step through the door beneath the coat of arms and, at the end of a corridor whose floor is tiled with Delft faience, you'll be surprised to find a very small garden full of flowers (*hof*) surrounded by tiny houses once home to elderly people in need. This former Beguine convent was founded in 1616. Today it's one of the most sought-after places in the city and a house here is cripplingly expensive.

❻ 't Smalle★★
Egelantiersgracht, 12
☎ 623 96 17.

This café, a Jordaan institution typical of the district, has been open since 1780, so the nicotine has had more than enough time to impregnate its walls and furniture. Note the pretty enamelled stained-glass windows and polished tables and chairs. Queen Beatrix herself came here to sample the cosy atmosphere, but she stayed outside on the floating terrace, which is set out at the first hint of sunny weather.

❼ Greenpeace★
Corner of Keizersgracht and Leliegracht.

The ecological organisation Greenpeace is housed in this very fine Art Nouveau building designed by Gerrit van Arkel and dating from 1905. The imposing façade is enlivened with mosaics, bow windows and pinnacles. Have a look too at the entrance hall, which is decorated with ceramics.

❽ Hieronymus Bosch★
Leliegracht, 36
☎ **623 71 78**
Open Mon.-Sat.
11.30am-5.30pm.

This narrow space, lined with shelves groaning with books from floor to ceiling, is one of the best bookshops in town, specialising in the medieval and Renaissance periods. You'll find everything to interest you here, from collectors' editions to popular books on the zodiac.

❾ Claes Claeszhofje
Egelantiersstraat, 28.

Step through the wooden door and you'll find yourself in one of Jordaan's secret places, a former hospice founded by a rich draper in 1616. Today's lucky residents are all students at the conservatory of music, which has taken the place over. The little adjoining restaurant serves generous portions of unpretentious food, to the accompaniment of singing at weekends.

❿ Noordermarkt★

On Monday mornings there is a bric-a-brac market here and on Saturday mornings a very picturesque market. Homing pigeons, exotic birds and cages full of cheeping chicks are ranged alongside stalls selling fresh farm produce.

⓫ Brouwersgracht ★★

The brewers' canal marks the northernmost edge of this district. With its many bridges, red-shuttered warehouses converted into lofts and flower-covered houseboats moored all along the quaysides, this is one of the most picturesque views in Amsterdam.

⑫ Gitanos★
Tweede Anjeliersdwarstraat, 3
☎ **639 25 87**
Mon., Wed., Fri. and Sat. noon-6pm.

A little shop specialising in rather kitsch religious bric-a-brac. Life-size St Theresas, embroidered chasubles, devout images of the Virgin Mary and baby Jesus, loads of stopwatches and incense-holders in the style of Ancient Egyptian perfume jars, in other words just the place to restore your faith.

⑬ 't Papeneiland★★
Prinsengracht, 2
☎ **624 19 89.**

Gleaming beer pumps, an old cast iron stove in the middle of the room and walls lined with Delft tiles make up the decor of this little 'brown café', which has had a loyal local clientele since 1642.

⑭ Koevoet★
Lindenstraat, 17
☎ **624 08 46**
Dinner after 6pm, except Mon.

An unpretentious little *eetcafé* of the kind that flourishes so busily all over Jordaan. The entrance is through an old bar with a well-worn floor, then up some steps to the small restaurant itself,

⑮ VAN WEES *JENEVER*★

Driehoeckstraat, at the very end of Brouwersgracht, is home to the oldest distillery in the country, owned by the van Wees family who, from generation to generation, have passed down the secret of making a *jenever* flavoured with herbs. If you want to sample the product, however, you have to keep going a little further, to the 'De Admiral' *proeflokaal* at Herengracht, 319.

where you'll find a few welcoming buffet tables set out.

⑯ Northern Church (Noorderkerk)
This is the Western Church's smaller sister-church, and was designed by the same architect. It was specially built for the Protestant inhabitants of Jordaan, who found the Westerkerk too posh for their comfort. This is one of the few churches where services are still held.

Rembrandtplein:
art by day, clubs by night

By day this district between the Amstel and Keizersgracht is a place of lovely squares and shady canals whose still waters mirror the magnificent façades of patrician residences, some of which may deign to open their doors and secrets to passers-by.

But once the strings of lights between the seven bridges of Reguliersgracht are switched on, the night people invade the streets and the area reveals its hip and trendy side, full of fast food outlets and gay bars.

❶ Rembrandtplein ★

The establishments on this square range from the posh Schiller café to topless bars, typifying the Jekyll and Hyde nature of this district, which is both extremely classy and highly dubious. Former host to the old butter market, the square was renamed after the great 17th-century master, whose statue stands in its centre.

❷ Van Loon Museum★★★
Keizersgracht, 672
☎ 624 52 55
Open Fri.-Mon. 11am-5pm.
Entry charge.

The heir to the Van Loon fortune has opened the doors of his family residence, inviting you into the cosseted world of the 18th-century patrician. With its silk-lined rooms, chests of tropical wood, family portraits and tables displaying valuable porcelain, this is one of the city's most delightful places.

❸ Hooghoudt★★
Reguliersgracht, 11
☎ **420 40 41**
Open every day 4pm-1am.

Once the office day is finished, this *proeflokaal* housed in an old 17th-century warehouse fills up and doesn't empty until closing-time. Here they drink Groningen *jenever*, which is kept in earthenware jars to preserve its special flavour. Start by ordering an iced *korenwijn* (wheat wine).

❹ Collection Six★★
Amstel, 218
☎ **673 21 21**
Private collection. Visit by appointment only, with tickets bought from the Rijksmuseum.

Admirably located on the Amstel, this elegant house is still inhabited by the descendants of the Six, who were Huguenot refugees from Saint-Omer in France. They were art-lovers who acquired one of the finest collections of 17th-century paintings, including exceptional works by Rembrandt and Frans Hals.

❺ Het Tuynhuys★
Reguliersdwarsstraat, 28
☎ **627 66 03**
Open Mon.-Fri. noon-2.30pm, every day 6.30-10.30pm.

A former carriage-shed hiding behind the flower market, designed by the photographer and interior designer Kees Hageman. In summer you eat in the beautiful garden to the sound of a flute. The very tempting set meals and varied à la carte menu change with the seasons.

❻ Willet Holthuysen Museum★★
Herengracht, 605
☎ **523 18 70**
Open Mon.-Fri. 10am-5pm, Sat. and Sun. 11am-5pm. Entry charge.

The Willet Holtuysens, a couple who lived in this beautiful 17th-century residence, were keen collectors of glassware, porcelain, silverware and paintings. Experience the daily life of the wealthy

❼ SATURNIO★
Reguliersdwarsstraat, 5
☎ **639 01 02**
Open every day noon-midnight.

A theatrical decor of columns and Moorish mosaics frequented by, among others, the gay community. Sicilian cuisine with delicious escalopes and fish specialities. Dishes of the day are written up on the blackboard.

18th-century bourgeoisie, from kitchen to formal garden.

❽ Tuschinski cinema★★
Reguliersbreestraat, 26-28
☎ **626 15 10**
Programmes start at noon.

See a film in screen 1 of this large theatre (original version with Dutch subtitles), if only for its beauty, and try to get a ground floor box. Otherwise just try to see the foyer and façade of this stunning Art Deco cinema buried in a street of fast food outlets.

Herengracht:
untouched by time

This peaceful canal, lined with magnificent old houses, is the most beautiful in Amsterdam. Its grand residences, whose Baroque pediments and severe façades reflect the character of their wealthy occupants, were designed and decorated by the best artists. To protect the inhabitants' peace, this has always been a strictly residential quarter, where restaurants and cafés have been permitted only on the intersecting streets. As a result this district has remained untouched by time or change and you'll find yourself listening out for the sound of hooves and carriage wheels on the street or the echoes of grand royal parties.

❶ ABN-AMRO bank★
Vijzelstraat, 66-80.

Yet another illustration of the architectural exuberance that reigned in Amsterdam in the 1920s. This strictly geometrical, multicoloured building, 100m/109 yds long and ten stories high, was designed by K. de Bazel.

❷ Katten Kabinet ★★
Herengracht, 497
☎ **626 53 78**
Open 28 Jun.-28 Aug. Tue.-Fri. 10am-2pm, Sat.-Sun. 1-5pm. Entry charge.

Cats rule in this fine residence from the 17th-century golden age, with its painted stucco decorations. Not only are they the subject of all temporary exhibitions held here, you'll find live examples curled up in a period armchair or gambolling about the garden.

❸ Golden Bend★★ (*Gouden bocht*)
Herengracht, 507, 495, 475, 476 and 478.

At the bend in the canal, you'll find a group of houses that are among the grandest in Amsterdam. Each one occupies a double plot and their proud, rather cold façades reflect the wealth and self-assurance of the patricians and merchants of the 18th century.

❹ Theater Museum ★★
Herengracht, 168
☎ 551 33 00
Open Tue.-Fri. 11am-5pm,
Sat. and Sun. 1-5pm.
Entry charge.

Make sure you see the city's finest monumental staircase. It spirals upwards with a false perspective in a hall that's entirely decorated in stucco and grisaille pictures with mythological themes by Jacob de Wit, an artist sought after by all the wealthy 18th-century bourgeoisie. The museum's other jewel is a miniature theatre (1781) with moving sets.

❻ Pompadour★
Huidenstraat, 12
☎ 623 95 54
Open Tue.-Fri. 9.30am-
5.45pm, Sat. 8.30am-
5.30pm.

Wealthy Amsterdammers come here to buy Pompadour's own luxury cakes, chocolates and

❺ Riviera★
Herenstraat, 2-6
☎ 622 76 75
Open Mon.-Fri. 9am-6pm,
Sat. 9am-5pm,
Sun. noon-5pm.

This is a world of plants, enriched with the subtle scents of flowers with delicate petals, a garden out of the thousand-and-one nights, recreated in this beautiful shop selling flowers and outdoor furniture, where you're bound to find some great ideas for home decoration.

caramels. The adjoining tea-house is always packed out in the afternoon, when the ladies take a break from shopping to renew their energies.

❼ d'Theeboom
Singel, 210
☎ 623 84 20
Dinner after 6pm.

The French owner is also the chef in this old cheese and butter warehouse. The menu varies according to what's available, with a few musts, such as cinnamon ice-cream and ice-cream with warm amarena cherries. Sheer delight!

❽ Deco sauna★
Herengracht, 115
☎ 623 82 15
Open Mon.-Sat. 10am-8pm.

If you really want to make yourself sweat, it's probably more pleasant to do it in beautiful surroundings. Here every single room is decorated with authentic 1920s artefacts. The magnificent stained glass, wood-panelling and wall and stair lamps were all bought from a large store in Paris, which was undergoing major renovation.

Antiques and bric-a-brac: where to go and what to look for

As you move from one canal to the next and from street to street, you'll find each is a little world in itself, with its own particular qualities, from the sure, unchanging values of the eighty antique dealers who have been located in Nieuwe Spiegelstraat since the opening of the Rijksmuseum, to the more basic pleasures offered by the restaurants and theatres around Leidseplein, where there's always something going on, day and night, via Prinsengracht, where divisions aren't so strict and you'll find antique dealers can find a home among the bric-a-brac shops, so long as they're prepared to show a bit of originality and a sense of humour.

❶ Couzijn Simon★★
Prinsengracht, 578
☎ 624 76 91
Open every day 10am-6pm.

Couzijn has two passions: his bright orange moustache and

very rare old toys. This 18th-century chemist's shop, with its floor of polished tiles, is now occupied by dolls with hair made of silk thread, rocking horses, sailing boats, tea-sets for dolls' parties and clockwork dogs.

❷ Frans Leidelmeijer★★
Nieuwe Spiegelstraat, 58
☎ 625 46 27
Open Mon.-Sat. noon-6pm.

Make sure you ring the bell and take a look at the Art Nouveau and Art Deco decor

of what is, indisputably, one of the area's most beautiful antique shops. Frans Leidelmeijer, author of a book on the subject, can tell you all about the furniture and objects designed by Berlage and the Amsterdam school.

❸ Metz & Co★
Keizersgracht, 455 (corner of Leidsestraat)
☎ 624 88 10
Open Mon.-Sat. 9.30am-6pm, Thu. 9pm, Sun. noon-5pm.

This large, very exclusive and very expensive store sells

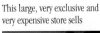

only top-of-the-range products, preferably British brands for table decoration. Every piece of furniture is signed — you might find a red and blue zig-zag chair by Rietveld for example. Under the dome by the same designer, you can have a brunch of salmon and toast, while enjoying the marvellous view of Amsterdam.

❹ American Café★★
Leidsekade, 97
☎ 624 53 22
Open 10-1am, Sun. brunch from 11.30am.

With the golden light pouring through its stained-glass windows, Tiffany chandeliers and lovely frescoes on the walls, this is the most authentic Art Deco setting

❺ A LA PLANCHA★
Eerste Looiersdwarsstraat, 15
☎ 420 36 33
Tue.-Sun. noon-midnight.

If the enormous bull's head hanging behind the bar doesn't put you off, slip up onto one of the high stools to choose from the home-made tapas or grilled gambas displayed behind the glass counter. Wash it all down with rough wine to the sound of Spanish hits. The temperature rises on Friday and Saturday nights, along with the sound of guitars.

you'll find in all Amsterdam to have a coffee or club sandwich and read the paper at the big reading table.

❻ De Melkweg★★
Lijnbaansgracht, 234a
☎ 624 17 77
Shows at 9.30pm.

In the 1970s this former dairy was an obligatory stop on the road to Katmandu. People with long hair, fringed jeans and long dresses would lie around together on the cushions in clouds of incense and marijuana smoke to the sound of an Indian sitar. The hippies have gone now but the Melkweg remains one of Amsterdam's most important music venues.

❼ De rare Kiek★★★
Prinsengracht, 539
☎ 620 98 60
Open Fri. and Sat. 1-6pm.

This is the lair of a real character who has spent much of his life in Africa and drinks *jenever* like water. His name is Ger and he has hundreds of fetishes, masks, statuettes and jewellery from Africa and the Pacific in an old warehouse full of nooks and crannies. Collectors and museum curators have begun to take an interest, so go and see them before it's too late.

The museum quarter: from Rembrandt to the avant-garde

A s well as being home to two of the city's most famous museums (the Museumplein is in the process of being transformed into a quiet park), this area also contains the popular Vordelpark. A haven of greenery in the heart of Amsterdam, there are trendy cafés and free concerts and shows in the open air theatre during the summer months.

Overtoom
Vondel
Vondelpark
Huygens Straat
Hobbemastr.
Hooft Straat
P. C. Hooft
Van Baerle Straat
Straat Paul Potter Straat
Rijks Museum ①
② **Van Gogh Museum**
③ **Stedelijk Museum**
Museum Straat
④ ⑤ **Concertgebouw**
CONCERTGEBOUW PLEIN
Straat
⑥
⑦

❶ National museum★★★ (Rijksmuseum)
Stadhouderskade, 42
☎ **673 21 21**
Entrance on south wing (department of Asiatic art), Hobbemastraat, 19
Open every day 10am–5pm
Entry charge.

This collection, with Rembrandt's *Night Watch* at its centre, is a kind of family

album of Dutch painting, including works by Vermeer, Frans Hals and many other masters who specialised in genre paintings, still lifes and landscapes. Don't miss the new exhibition of Asiatic art in the south wing or the exquisite collection of dolls houses *(poppenhuizen)*.

❷ Van Gogh Museum★★★
Paulus Potterstraat, 7
☎ **570 52 91**
Every day 10am–5pm (closed until May 99, finest works are in the Rijksmuseum).

The Dutch have the most complete collection of this extraordinary and well-loved

This museum, re-opened in June 1999 after renovations and the building of a new exhibition wing, houses some 200 paintings and 550 sketches. They show Van Gogh in all his moods, from the sombre tones

of the potato-eaters of Brabant, to the bright yellows and blues of Provence, and taken to extremes in the reds and blacks of his *Wheatfield with crows*.

❸ City Museum★★ (Stedelijk Museum)
Paulus Potterstraat, 13
☎ 573 29 11

Open every day 11am-5pm, 1 Apr.-30 Sep. 10am-6pm. Entry charge.

This showcase for modern and contemporary art is above all an active centre for avant-

garde works. Its collections are constantly being enriched and its many exhibitions include both retrospectives and presentations by young, unknown artists.

❹ Café Welling ★
J.W. Brouwersstraat, 32
☎ 662 01 55
Open 4pm-1am, Fri.-Sat. 2am.

The pavement behind the Concertgebouw fills with tables as soon as the first ray of sunlight is spotted. This is the 'brown café' of the young and hip. The musicians have their own special table.

❺ Concertgebouw ★★★
Concertgebouwplein, 2-6
☎ 573 05 73
Open 10am-7pm
Concerts begin at 8.15pm.

In 1888 a new concert hall was built on piles at the heart of the residential districts, then under construction. The neo-Classical façade hides an auditorium

❻ Hollandse Manege★★
Vondelstraat, 140
☎ 618 09 42
Open 8.30am-1pm, Sun. until 5pm.

Step through the heavy gate and the musky smell of working horses assails your nostrils. The ring has an imperial box and a metal roof, and is staggeringly large. Its design was based on that of the Spanish Riding School in Vienna. Riders and horses have been trained here since 1882.

with exceptional acoustics, which have given the hall its great reputation. The Concertgebouw is also famous for its orchestra of early instruments.

❼ Brasserie van Baerle★★
Van Baerlestraat, 158
☎ 679 15 32
Open noon-11pm, Sun. from 10a∙1
Closed Sat.

The young-at-heart mingle with music-lovers in this very classy Art Deco brasserie. The shady garden is a boon in summer, as are the salads. The menu, with its hint of nouvelle cuisine, changes with the seasons. The most popular place in town for a light lunch or supper.

Plantage: dreams of far away

Far from the city's noise, elegant villas and shady avenues give this very green district an unexpected charm. You could almost forget you're in Amsterdam if the sea weren't so close. It's here that the city's inhabitants have locked away their dreams of faraway lands beyond the sea, in institutions that tell of the peoples and plants of the former colonies of the Dutch East India company.

Ooster

Prins Hendrikkade

Seafaring Museum ⑥

Kattenburger Straat

⑤

Shippers Gracht

Nieuwevaart

KADIJKS PLEIN

④ **Entrepotdok**

Berlage's Fortress

Muldersstr. *Nieuwe Heren Gracht* *Plantage Parklaan* ① *H. Polak laan* *Plantage* *Entrepot dok*

② *Dok Laan*

Hortus Botanicus *Plantage Kerklaan* *Artis* ③

Plantage Middenlaan

Plantage *Muider* *Gracht*

ALEXANDER PLEIN

⑦

Tropical Museum

Oosterpark

❶ Berlage's 'fortress'★★★ (Burcht van Berlage)
Henri Polaklaan, 9
☎ 624 11 66
**Open Tue.-Fri. 11am-5pm,
Sun. 1-5pm
Entry charge.**

This headquarters of the union of diamond-cutters and merchants is one of the finest buildings by Berlage, who designed it in 1900 in the spirit of socialism. The severity of the façade, symbolising the strength of working people, contrasts with the light that floods the interior, growing more and more intense as you move up the yellow stairwell, which is lit by a cascade of multi-faceted lamps.

❷ Hortus Botanicus★★
Plantage Middenlaan, 2a
☎ 625 84 11
**Open Mon.-Fri. 9am-4pm,
Sat. and Sun. 11am-4pm
Entry charge.**

It was the VOC (East India Company) which set up a garden of medicinal herbs in 1682. Exotic plants brought from the colonies, such as coffee and spices, were gradually acclimatised here. Essential to see are the orangery, a palm house containing a cycad four hundred years old and greenhouses maintaining different climates.

❸ Artis★★
Plantage Kerklaan, 40
☎ 523 34 00
Open every day 9am-5pm. Entry charge.

The city's largest garden is also home to the zoo, whose many inhabitants include big cats, flamingos, polar bears and sea-lions. There's also a reptile house, an aviary with macaws and multicoloured parrots and an aquarium with different tanks filled with fresh or salt water, containing a total of 500 species of fish and marine animals. Like the ocean only smaller.

❹ Entrepotdok★
Entrance on Kadijksplein.

Step through the monumental door bearing the initials VOC and you'll find an astounding array of 84 warehouses, each bearing

the name of a town where the East India Company had a trading post and arranged in alphabetical order. These have now been converted into flats, offices and some restaurants, such as the Saudade, which serves Portuguese food.

❺ ABOARD A VOC THREE-MASTER★★

The *Amsterdam*, built in 1990 and moored in front of the arsenal, is a faithful reproduction of a three-master owned by the Dutch East India Company (VOC.) in the 18th century. If you go aboard, you'll gain a better understanding of the feat of physical, mental and spiritual strength needed by a crew of 300 to live for months and indeed years in such a confined space, a prey to scurvy and the elements. Not for the faint-hearted.

❻ Seafaring Museum★★★ (Scheepvaart Museum)
Kattenburgplein, 1
☎ 523 22 22
Open Tue.-Sun. 11am-5pm, Jun.-Sep. also open Mon. Entry charge.

Relive the extraordinary adventures of the brave sailors who set forth across the seven seas in this former Admiralty arsenal. Three floors of models, navigation charts and instruments retrace the maritime history of the Netherlands. The royal launch, built in 1816 for King William III and decorated with gold leaf, is the star attraction of the exhibition.

❼ Tropical Museum★★ (Tropen Museum)
Linnaeusstraat, 2
☎ 568 82 15
Open Mon.-Fri. 10am-5pm, Sat. and Sun. noon-5pm Entry charge.

Beneath the glass dome of this very fine colonial building, you can travel across half the planet in less than an hour, plunging by turns into the cacophony of a Bombay street, the bustle of an Arab souk or the everyday business of an African village. You can also find out about different types of music from around the world.

Around Centraal Station: *site of the old port*

Although the city of Amsterdam is built on an artificial island, the central station resolutely turns its back on the sea. Yet move away from the torrent of bicycles, trams and pedestrians rumbling up to the Dam, and you'll find islands covered in warehouses, with battered old craft moored alongside.

❶ Centraal Station★★

In 1869 this building, 300m/328yds long and solidly anchored in the sea by means of 8,687 piles, was a real challenge for P.J.H. Cuypers, the architect who designed the Rijksmuseum. Inside, on platform 2, you'll discover his secret garden, the royal waiting-room, and the *Eerste Klas* restaurant, with its Belle Époque decor.

❷ Restaurant Pier 10★★
De Ruyterkade-Steiger, 10
☎ 624 82 76
Open every day after 6.30pm (credit cards not accepted).

If you cross the central station, you'll find an old customs house, very small and apparently standing on the water, all by itself at the end of

platform 10, the line to the docks. Make sure you book a table in the rotunda and arrive before night falls so you can enjoy the view over the port and the Ij. Generous portions and a warm, friendly ambiance.

❸ Oininio★★
Prins Hendrikkade, 20-21
☎ 553 93 22
Open every day after 10am.

Formerly 'Oibibio' (the photo shows the old name) the owner has created a

'meditation centre'. Starting from the ground floor, you'll find a vegetarian café-restaurant (not to everyone's taste, but superb decor), a Japanese teahouse and a sauna. In the basement there are various sections selling everything to do with ecology, relaxation and esotericism from Jesus to Buddha.

❹ Interpolm Amsterdam
Prins Hendrikkade, 11
☎ 627 77 50
Mon. 1-6pm, Tue.-Fri. 10am-6pm, Sat. 10am-5pm.

Want to find out all about *KC 33*, *Swiss XT* or *California Skunk*? No, nothing to do with computers, these are marijuana seeds, specially selected to be grown at home. Here you'll find all the information, advice and equipment you need to grow this rather special plant (which is, let's not forget, totally illegal in most countries outside Holland).

❺ The Spanish House★ (De Spaanse Gevel)

This café at no. 2 Singel, the canal which encircled the medieval city, has a lovely façade dated 1650, a stepped gable and a coat of arms

showing a wheelbarrow. This was where the mail left for The Hague and the great merchant ships docked for unloading after passing through the lock.

❻ De Gouden Reael restaurant★
Zandhoek, 14
☎ 623 38 83
Closed Sun.
No lunch on Sat.

The dock that faces the sea on Reaalneiland was the place where they used to unload sand (*Zand*). Nowadays the

❼ PRINSENEILAND★

This island, far from the expensive 17th-century districts and linked to dry land by elegant draw-bridges, used to be covered in warehouses and factories making rope and tar. When these closed the squatters moved in. It has now become a very desirable area, with its warehouses all turned into luxury flats.

people who come ashore here tend to be owners of traditional old boats looking forward to eating some good French regional cuisine in this restaurant in a converted 17th-century house.

❽ West Indischehuis★
Haarlemmerstraat, 75.

This house, with its pretty façade, used to be the headquarters of the renowned India Company, not to be confused with its rival, the VOC (East India Company). Today it's a municipal hall and people's university. In the middle of the central courtyard stands a statue of Peter Stuyvesant, governor of New Amsterdam.

De Pijp: a cosmopolitan atmosphere

Amsterdam also has its own immigrants' quarter. The main residents of this district to the south of the 17th-century city are from Turkey, Morocco, Surinam or Indonesia. However, unlike immigrants to many other European capitals, they're able to coexist peacefully with young Dutch couples, who are also drawn to the low-rent social housing schemes. The most successful of these are undoubtedly those designed in the 1920s by architects of the Amsterdam school. Elsewhere narrow streets and cramped houses have earned this district the unflattering name of 'pipe' (*pijp*).

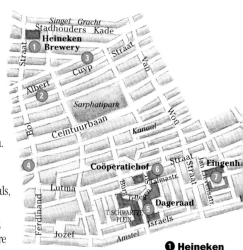

❶ Heineken brewery★★
Stadhouderskade, 78 (corner of F. Bolstraat)
☎ 523 96 66
Mon.-Fri. guided tours 9.30am, 11am, 1pm and 2.30pm, Sat. in Jul. and Aug. Entry charge.

The most famous of the Dutch breweries has moved to a more modern factory, but the old building has been converted into a beer museum. The 2-hour guided tour takes you through the vast brewing rooms, retracing the story of this ancient drink, which was known to the Egyptian pharaoh Khufu and his subjects over 4,500 years ago. Free tasting!

❷ Albert Cuypmarkt★
Albert Cuypstraat Mon.-Sat. 10am-4.30pm.

Since 1905 this has been the most frequented, popular and

'Amsterdam, Turkish, Christian, Pagan, Jewish. Reservoir of sects and crucible of schisms, this bank of conscience where every opinion, however strange, is given credit and value.'

Marwell.

cosmopolitan of the city's markets. It has around three hundred stalls stretching 2km/1 mile and selling clothes, fabrics by the metre, fish, cheese, flowers, fruit and vegetables, all at the lowest prices.

❸ Gerard Dou★
A. Cuypstraat, 217-219
☎ 400 43 26
Open Mon.-Sat. 9am-6pm.

Everything is for sale in this huge warehouse hidden behind the stallholders' displays – rustic wardrobes, large mirrors, display cases, mahogany writing desks, Chinese boxes, knick-

knacks and ice-skates, all for really good prices. If you look very carefully you're bound to find some rare treasure.

❹ Gambrinus★
Ferdinand Bolstraat, 180
☎ 671 73 89
Open every day 11am-1pm.

A real 'brown café', still there among the

Surinamese and Turkish restaurants and always very lively after 6pm, particularly at the weekend. This is also a good place in the area to eat Dutch food.

❺ Dageraad★★★
P.L. Takstraat.

In 1921 a socialist building cooperative asked two architects, M. de Klerk and P.L. Kramer, to draw up plans for 350 workers' housing

units. The two brick buildings on the corner of P.L. Takstraat sum up the philosophy of the Amsterdam school, which advocated rigour, verticality and colour in designs combining utilitarianism with beauty.

❻ Coöperatiehof★
Entrance on Talmastraat.

In the Dutch tradition of the *bof*, a kind of courtyard surrounded by housing for the needy, this symmetrical group is dominated not by a church but by the bell tower of the public library. The books and key on the façade are symbols of the emancipation of the working class through knowledge.

❼ Eigen Haard★★
Smaragdplein.

Another remarkable scheme designed by the Amsterdam school for the Eigenhaard (Home) cooperative in 1917. The school and social housing are all rigorously symmetrical in design, softened by the tawny shades of the brick, which has been used in a whimsical, playful manner.

Rooms and restaurants
Practicalities

Amsterdam is comparatively small, so your main concerns when choosing a hotel will be price and location. Avoid the central station area and the red light district unless you like noise and unsavoury characters. The hotels outside these two areas are easy to get to by tram or taxi, or even on foot, if you aren't too heavily loaded.

HOTELS

The luxury hotels have reduced rates at weekends, particularly if you book through a travel agent, although this may mean you don't get such a good room. There are also many very quiet and comfortable hotels near Vondelpark. The (very large) breakfast is usually included in the price. Low season prices apply from the end of November to the end of April, and also in July and August.

You're not usually expected to leave a tip, unless you're staying in a luxury hotel, where you

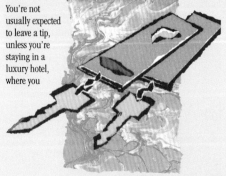

should tip messenger boys and chambermaids.

Hotels in Amsterdam are classified according to international standards. There's an enormous amount of choice; however you should remember that a hotel's star rating is based on objective criteria, such as whether or not it has a lift, or televisions in the rooms. So in the 2 and 3 star categories, you'll find

BOOKING A HOTEL

Most hotels are affiliated to the NRC (Nederlands Reserverings Centrum).
☎ (70) 320 25 00 / 419 55 44
🅕 (70) 320 26 11.
A free booking service is provided by the Tourist Information Office, where you'll be dealt with by someone who speaks English. You'll find brochures giving prices and desciptions of hotels in every branch of these offices.

excellent old-style hotels in former patrician houses, where the atmosphere tends to be warmer and more welcoming. These are the hotels we prefer to recommend.

In you're going in spring – particularly April or May – or September, it's a good idea to book several weeks in advance. This is even more important if you've chosen a nice little old-style hotel with a view of the canal. You can book by telephone or fax using a credit card – don't forget to include your address and card number when booking by fax. Postal orders and eurocheques are also accepted for payment. If you fail to take up your reservation, you'll be charged a cancellation fee corresponding to the price of one night at the hotel.

RESTAURANTS

The Dutch like to economise and don't often eat out. Restaurants are generally the preserve of businessmen and tourists and can be very expensive if you pick from the à la carte menu. For this reason, the great majority of restaurants offer more reasonably-priced set meals of between 3 and 5 courses.

Prices as shown include a 15% service charge. The Dutch seldom leave a tip, though they may round up the bill to the nearest florin or ten florins. If you do feel you want to leave a tip in a restaurant, you shouldn't make it more than 10Fl.

Lastly, remember that the Dutch eat early. Restaurants are open from 6pm and the kitchen usually closes at 10pm. A few places around the Concertgebouw, Leidseplein and Rembrandtplein stay open until midnight. However the most sensible thing is always to call first and book if you want to

make sure you don't wind up in McDonald's.

Our selections are largely based on value for money.

TYPICAL DISHES

Typical Dutch food is sturdy winter food, like *'stamppot'*: mashed potato mixed with vegetables (cabbage or endive) and meat, often fried bacon or minced meat. Another national dish is the Dutch pancake (sweet or savoury fillings), which is so filling that you can eat it as a meal. Most restaurants nowadays serve 'modern' food; a combination of cuisines from all over the world. There are

some old fashioned restaurants that serve traditional Dutch food, but they are mostly visited by tourists. Those showing the *Neerlands Dis* logo all serve traditional cuisine. All these restaurants will have an English version of their menu. Indonesian food is very popular in Holland since Indonesia was once a Dutch colony.

ACTIVE OR PASSIVE SMOKING?

ROKEN VERBODEN

As yet, there is no anti-smoking legislation in the Netherlands, which means that very few restaurants or cafés have no-smoking zones.

In cafés you can often order snacks like a cheese platter, 'vlammetjes' or 'bitterballen'. Jenever (Dutch version of gin) is the national drink. A late night favourite is 'eating out of the wall' in brightly lit snack bars called 'Febo' where the deep fried snacks are displayed and kept hot in individual vending machines. During the day, you can eat on the street at various fish stalls where you can try the famous raw herring or other smoked or fried fish. See page 124 for a list of other Dutch dishes and tips on understanding the menu.

HOTELS

Near the Béguinage

Esthera★★★

Singel, 303-309
☎ 624 51 46
𝔽 623 90 01
Trams 1, 2, 5.

Four old brick buildings near the flower market, renovated and very pretty. The breakfast room is decorated in dark shades, with typical Dutch wood panelling and the bedrooms are large and comfortable.

Near Leidseplein

American★★★★

Leidsekade, 97
☎ 624 53 22
𝔽 625 32 36
Trams 1, 2, 5, 11.

In the early 20th century the decor of this hotel, where Mata Hari consummated her eighth marriage, was pure Art Nouveau. Although the original decoration has gone from the pastel bedrooms with their large bathrooms, the famous Art Deco American Café is still *the* meeting-place for Amsterdam's intellectuals. The hotel has terraces on Leidseplein and, on the top floor, a fitness centre and 8-space car park.

Dikker & Thijs ★★★

Prinsengracht, 444
☎ 626 77 21
𝔽 625 89 86
Trams 1, 2, 5, 11.

A luxury establishment a stone's throw from Leidseplein. Unfortunately, recent restoration has removed all its Art Deco elements. Decorated in greys and pinks, with large bathrooms and

The flower-filled courtyard of the Pulitzer hotel

one of Amsterdam's really good restaurants, the Prinsenkelder, in the basement. There's a car park (not free) 100m/yds away. The bedrooms overlooking Prinsengracht are quieter.

Near Rembrandtplein

Seven Bridges★★

Reguliersgracht, 3
☎ 623 13 29
Tram 4.

A small, 8-room hotel by the most beautiful of the canals, whose owner, a secondhand dealer, has decorated it in a range of styles, from empire to Art Deco. Vases filled with flowers, Persian carpets and a big breakfast served in bed. Views over the garden or the canal, but the staircase is steep. An excellent hotel.

Prinsenhof★

Prinsengracht, 810
☎ 623 17 72
𝔽 638 33 68
Tram 4.

Small, tastefully-decorated hotel near Frederiksplein

and the friendly cafés of Utrechtsestraat, which would suit those on limited budgets who don't mind steep stairs. Book in advance if you want one of the 2 bedrooms with an en-suite shower. 5% additional charge for credit cards.

Jordaan

Pulitzer★★★★★

Prinsengracht, 315-331
☎ 523 52 35
𝔽 627 67 53
Trams 13, 14, 17.

Views of the canal or the courtyard garden of this unusual hotel occupying a block of 27

bourgeois residences between Prinsengracht and Keizersgracht. Clients generally businessmen and conference participants. Good location close to Jordaan. Inexpensive nouvelle cuisine in the *Café Pulitzer* and the gourmet restaurant in a former chemist's shop, *De Goudsbloem*. For real style, arrive by boat.

Canal House★★★

Keizersgracht, 148
☎ 622 51 82 **F** 624 13 17.
Trams 13, 17.

The best-designed of the small, old-style hotels. Intimate 17th-century decor in a beautiful house on the edge of Jordaan. Crystal chandeliers, freshly-cut flowers, period furniture and antiques. Book two months in advance.

Toren★★★

Keizersgracht, 164
☎ 622 63 52
F 626 97 05
Trams 13, 17.

Situated on one of the most beautiful canals, this hotel is comfortable and welcoming. Ask for a room overlooking either the canal or the small, Laura Ashley-style house in the garden (room 111). Special offers for three nights during the winter. Characterful bar with old woodwork.

Acacia★

Lindengracht, 251
☎ 622 14 60
F 638 07 48.
A small hotel with 14 rooms and a very Dutch feel, run by a young couple. En-suite bathrooms in every room and a large breakfast included in the price. For something different, try one of

the rooms in the hotel's two houseboats on the nearby canal. Very popular, so booking is a must. Add 5% to the bill for payment by credit card.

Herengracht

Ambassade★★★

Herengracht, 341
☎ 626 23 33
F 624 53 21
Trams 1, 2, 5.

The favourite hotel of authors Michel Tournier and Umberto Eco, this is the most luxurious of the old-style hotels, occupying eight fine 17th-century houses.

Period furniture and interesting and unusual decor in the public areas. A choice of top-floor bedrooms under the rafters or very large rooms overlooking the canal. So quiet you can hear the ducks quacking. Twenty-four-hour restaurant service.

The Ambassade Hotel on Herengracht

Keizershof ★
Keizersgracht, 618
☎ **622 28 55**
F **624 84 12**
Trams 16, 24, 25.

An authentic 17th-century building, where Mrs de Vries makes you feel at home in a typically Dutch setting. Six pleasant rooms with period furniture and old-fashioned linen. In good weather breakfast is served in the flower-filled garden and there's a piano in the sitting-room.

Plantage

Amstel Inter-Continental
★★★★★
Prof. Tulpplein, 1
☎ **622 60 60**
F **622 58 08**
Metro Weesperplein or trams 6, 7, 10.

This luxury hotel, built in 1867 and restored at great expense, offers its wealthy clients a personalised service. The 79 rooms are full of surprises, from the expensive furniture and silk sheets to the crystal carafes in the bar and a bathroom fit for a film star. Other features include supervised parking, heated swimming-pool, sauna, Turkish bath, limousines and gourmet restaurant, La Rive, with its terrace by the Amstel.

Near Centraal Station

New York ★★
Herengracht, 13
☎ **624 30 66**
F **620 32 30.**

At the northern end of Herengracht and a stone's throw

from the central station. Popular with both gay men and women. Very modern and clean, with marble and mirrors on every floor. Small private garage. Breakfast times to cater for late risers.

Rokin

De L'Europe
★★★★★
Nieuwe Doelenstraat, 2-8
☎ **531 17 77**
F **531 17 78**
Trams 4, 9, 14, 16, 24, 25.

This luxury hotel, with its great location in the heart of Amsterdam, was opened in 1896 and recently celebrated its centenary. Famous guests have included Elizabeth Taylor. The hotel combines refinement with personalised service and has an excellent restaurant, the Excelsior, a large waterside

terrace, a fitness centre with a small, Hollywood-style swimming pool and a private car park. Ask for a room with a balcony overlooking the Amstel

Agora ★
Singel, 462
☎ **627 22 00**
F **627 22 02**
Trams 4, 9, 14, 16, 24, 25.

This old building near the flower market has been nicely restored by two friends. The rooms overlooking the canal are noisier though more expensive. A lovely setting for your breakfast.

The museum quarter

Jan Luyken ★★★★
Jan Luykenstraat, 58
☎ **573 07 30**
F **676 38 41**
Trams 2, 3, 5, 12.

In a quiet street near Vondelpark, theatres and museums, the van Schaik family have turned three 19th-century patrician houses into a hotel. Quiet atmosphere, classic furniture, Art Nouveau decor and a warm welcome at an affordable price. Street parking possible but not free.

Toro★★★

Koningslaan, 64.
☎ 673 72 23
🄵 675 00 31
Tram 2.

An old patrician house 10 mins from the centre, next to Vondelpark, with 22 comfortable and deliciously quiet rooms. Features include a breakfast room open to the garden, terrace, antique furniture, oriental carpets and a warm welcome. There are many parking facilities available in the area. Excellent value for money.

Villa Borgmann
★★

Koningslaan, 48
☎ 673 52 52
🄵 676 25 80
Tram 2.

This small, peaceful and welcoming hotel, situated in the residential area by Vondelpark, has 15 rooms with en-suite showers, the best of which overlook the park. Furnished in cane and pastel tones. Parking available nearby.

De Filosoof★★

Anna Vodelstraat, 6
☎ 683 30 13
🄵 685 37 50.

This hotel near Vondelpark and the cinema museum has an original feature – the decor in each of its 25 rooms is based on a philosopher. You sleep under the watchful eye of Kant, Goethe, Marx, Dante or one of the great Japanese thinkers. Not that this means a lack of comfort – quite the opposite in fact. Breakfast in the garden in fine weather. A quality address.

The Toro hotel, amidst the greenery of the Vondelpark

RESTAURANTS

Near the Béguinage

Kantjil & De Tijger
★★

Spuistraat, 291-293
☎ 620 09 94
Trams 1, 2, 5
Open every day after
4.30pm.

A very fashionable Indonesian restaurant, despite unexciting decor. Serves many Javanese specialities, as well as the inevitable and very copious *rijsttafel*.

Haesje Claes★★

Spuitraat, 275
☎ 624 99 98
Trams 1, 2, 5
Open every day noon-10pm.

This restaurant sports the *Neerlands Dis* sign, indicating a typical Dutch establishment. Inside simple food is served in a warm and friendly

atmosphere. The *hollandse visbord,* an assortment of herrings, mackerel, shrimps and smoked eels, is a house speciality.

Dam

De Roode Leeuw
★★

Damrak, 93-94
☎ 555 06 66.
Open every day noon-10pm.

A traditional brasserie serving

Dutch meat and fish specialities. Vegetables in season – particularly asparagus – are cooked in a great variety of ways. Covered terrace on the busy Damrak.

Red light district

Hemelse Modder
★★

Oude Waal, 9
☎ 624 32 03
Bus 22
Every day except Mon.
6pm-1am

Indian, Italian, French and vegetarian dishes, tending towards nouvelle cuisine, are served in a simple setting overlooking the quiet canal. Three-course set meal at 42Fl. Restaurant run by former squatters who know how to cook. Very popular, so booking a must.

Wellcome★

Zeedijk, 57
☎ 638 62 34
Bus 22
Every day noon-11pm

The district's best Chinese restaurant specialising in very fresh seafood. Pleasant ambiance and chef's surprises, such as grilled oysters and steamed scallops.

Jordaan

Long Pura★★★

Rozengracht, 46-48
☎ 623 89 50
Trams 13, 14, 17
Thu.-Mon. 6-11pm.

Sublime decor of richly-coloured

fabrics through which actor-waiters glide. Serves authentic Balinese cuisine, very subtle and delicate, from *Makanan Nusantara* to stuffed duck with Indonesian spices.

Bordewijk★★★
Noordermarkt, 7
☎ 624 38 99
Evenings only. Closed Mon.

High-tech decor and background music, excellent cuisine varying according to what is on sale in the market at the time, with fish and game specialities. Booking a must for this very popular restaurant known for its wines.

Speciaal★★
Nieuwe Leliestraat, 142
☎ 624 97 06
Open every day after 5.30pm.

In the heart of Jordaan, with some of the best Indonesian food in Amsterdam, the decor hasn't changed for 15 years. Try the excellent 'rice table' *(rijsttafel)*. Small eaters beware – the *rijsttafel* consists of a dozen dishes with two kinds of rice, so order one between two. Very relaxed atmosphere.

De Bak★
Prinsengracht, 193 (near Prinsenstraat)
☎ 625 79 72
Open every day 5-11pm.

Odd and very friendly – the basement of an old canal house transformed into a restaurant-car. Those who like good meat cooked on a charcoal grill should be sure not to miss this one. New set meal every day at 24Fl.

Toscanini★★
Lindengracht, 75
☎ 623 28 13
Tram 10. Open every day after 6pm. Booking advisable.

Converted factory boasting a beautiful interior and woman chef. Inexpensive gourmet dishes are cooked using fresh produce, the wine list is interesting and the atmosphere very warm and lively.

Jewish quarter

De Magere Brug★
Amstel, 81
☎ 622 65 02
Metro Waterlooplein.
Open every day from noon.
Kitchen closes at 9pm.

Small, unpretentious restaurant with a terrace opposite the *Magere Brug* ('Thin Bridge') over the Amstel. Particularly popular with Amsterdamers because of its home cooking at good prices. Snails, spare-ribs and veal liver are served along with herrings, eels and shrimps.

Rokin

Tom Yam★★
Staalstraat, 22
☎ 622 95 33
Trams 4, 9, 16, 24, 25
Evenings only.

Perfect service in a pleasing decor. The Thai cuisine has all the subtle flavours of citronella and coriander and is sometimes also very hot and spicy. Set meals from 40Fl, but for a minimum of two people only. Beware – the wines are very expensive!

Near Rembrandtplein

Sichuan Food
★★★★

Reguliersdwarsstraat, 35
☎ 626 93 27
Trams 16, 24, 25
Open every day 5pm-2am.

Authentic Chinese cuisine awarded stars by the gourmet guides. Absolutely must be tried, particularly the Sichuan specialities, which are often hot and spicy. Ask the owner to compose your meal for you, but expect to pay for it!

Le Pêcheur★★

Reguliersdwarsstraat, 32
☎ 624 31 21
Trams 16, 24, 25
Open Mon.-Fri. noon-midnight, Sat. 5pm-midnight, closed Sun.

A fine selection of fish and other seafood cooked the Italian way in a former shed. *Sashimi*, caviar, oyster and lobster snacks served until 1am. Eat in the garden in summer.

Near Leidseplein

Prinsenkelder★★★

Prinsengracht, 438
☎ 422 27 77
Trams 1, 2, 5, 11.

Cellar with an intimate atmosphere and sober black and white decor enlivened by exotic wood and large bouquets of

RESTAURANT DE PRINSENKELDER

flowers. Generous portions of imaginative Franco-Italian cuisine, accompanied by wines selected in France, Italy, Australia and South Africa. Not be be missed!

Tout court★★★

Runstraat, 13
☎ 625 86 37
Trams 1, 2, 5
Open every day until 11.30pm, no lunch at weekends.

Meeting-place of Amsterdam's high society. French cuisine lovingly prepared by John Fagel, one of the city's greatest chefs. Specialities include liver, kidneys and cold prepared pork . Booking a must.

Bento★★

Kerkstraat, 148
☎ 622 86 27
Trams 16, 24, 25
Open 5.30-10pm, except Mon.
Very Japanese decor of tatami mats and bamboo in which to eat healthy, balanced food served on appropriate dishes. Raw and cooked fish as well as vegetarian food.

Near Herengracht

Christophe★★★

Leliegracht, 46
☎ 625 08 07
Trams 13, 14, 17
Tue.-Sat. after 7pm.

Classic cuisine from south-west France, reinvented by French chef Jean-Christophe Royer. Very unusual decor by Dutch designer Paul van den Berg. Excellent wine list.

't Heertje★★

Herenstraat, 16
☎ 625 81 27
Trams 1, 2, 5
Thu.-Mon. after 5.30pm.

Not a wide choice, but the menu of subtle, imaginative cuisine changes every day, depending on the catch in the fishmonger's opposite, where the chef buys his ingredients. Traditional food also served. Only 8 tables, so it's best to book.

The museum quarter

Bodega Keyzer ★★★

Van Baerlestraat, 96
☎ 671 14 81
Trams 3, 12
Open noon-11.30 pm.

Classy diner favoured by musicians and music lovers from the Concertgebouw. The best sole meunière in town and a delicious fruit zabaglione. Booking essential.

Le Garage★★★

Ruysdaelstraat, 54-56
☎ 679 71 76
Trams 3, 5, 12
Open every day noon-2pm, 6-11pm.

Very fashionable. A garage transformed by the architect of the Stopera, frequented by those in the know. Red benches and mirrors where you can nibble at the slimming menu or try a few supposedly French specialities. In other words, the food isn't the main attraction. Booking essential.

Sama Sebo★★

P.C. Hoofstraat, 27
☎ 662 81 46
Bus 63
Open noon-10pm, closed Sun.

Affordable nasi goreng and bami goreng specialities and 23-dish *rijsttafel* near the Rijksmuseum. Very welcoming with pleasant decor.

Zabar's★★

Van Baerlestraat, 49
☎ 679 88 88
Trams 3, 5, 12
11am-1am, closed Sun.
No lunch Mon. or Sat.

Pretty interior open to a garden decorated in trompe-l'œil. Mediterranean cuisine for the greedy. A choice of *gazpacho, zarzuela, tajines* or *carpaccio* with delicious desserts. Mixed, but generally younger clientele.

Near Centraal Station

De Silveren Spiegel★★★

Kattengat, 4-6
☎ 624 65 89
Dinner from 6pm, not Sun.

Candlelit decor in 17th-century house. Warm welcome and highly inventive cuisine from starter to dessert, created by a gourmet chef who loves good French wines. Very affordable prices for one of Amsterdam's best restaurants. Booking advisable.

Eerste Klas★★

Stationplein, 15
☎ 625 01 31
9.30am-11pm, dinner 5-10pm

An oasis of peace amidst the hustle and bustle of the station. Next to the gilded gate of the Queen's waiting-room on platform 2B, the Four Seasons Saloon has been transformed into a superb brasserie serving traditional cuisine à la carte. Fin de siècle atmosphere.

LIGHT MEALS AND SNACKS

The Pancake Bakery

Prinsengracht, 191
☎ 625 13 33
Open noon-9.30pm.

If it's generous portions at nice prices you're after, here you

can choose from 40 kinds of savoury and sweet pancakes, for example a cheese and ginger pancake. It's always packed, so expect to wait.

Oininio

Prins Hendrikkade, 20-21
☎ 553 93 55.

Formerly 'Oibibio', this café-restaurant is on the first floor of the old Hotel Mercurius near the central station. You'll find a Japanese teahouse where you can drink tea in a timeless atmosphere.

Café Pulitzer

Prinsengracht, 315-331
☎ 523 52 35.

A chic eatery where you can try the dish of the day or just have a cup of tea and a delicious tart.

Small Talk

Van Baerlestraat, 52
☎ 671 48 64.

In the up-market part of town, very good tarts made on the premises and a good selection of teas. The terrace is rather noisy.

CAFÉS

Café Chris

Bloemstraat, 42
☎ 624 59 42.

Situated in Jordaan, near Westerkerk, this historic 'brown café' (1624) is a popular student haunt.

De Druif

Rapenburgerplein, 83
☎ 624 45 30 (near the Seafaring Museum).

A truly authentic Amsterdam café housed in a former *jenever* distillery, far from the tourist circuit in the former dockland area.

Het Molenpad

Prinsengracht, 653
☎ 625 96 80.

Photographic exhibitions and a very literary clientele in this lovely 'brown café'. Try some delicious *bitterballen* with your beer.

Café practicalities

If you sit out on the terrace, you'll be asked to pay immediately. Inside the 'brown cafés' the waiter will keep a record of what you have in his notebook. Over an evening, and lulled by a few *jenevers*, you can find yourself running up a sizable bill. You've been warned!

De Blincker

St Barberenstraat, 7
☎ 627 19 38.

Near the avant-garde theatres, a very trendy bar with a fine high-tech decor and a winter garden open in the late afternoon.

Luxembourg

Spui, 22 ☎ 620 62 64.

Marble, copper and polished woodwork set the tone of old-fashioned comfort. A meeting-place for yuppies and people from the advertising world after 5pm. The rest of the time the patrons are very young and hip.

Spanjer van Twist

Leliegracht, 60 ☎ 639 01 09.

Café overlooking a lovely shady canal, with tables set up outside as soon as the sun shines. The patrons tend to be young and resolutely non-conformist. Snacks and light meals served all day.

Finch

Noordermarkt, 5
☎ 626 24 61.

A pleasant little bistrot where the locals go for a glass of wine after the Saturday market or to eat the dish of the day.

THE *PROEFLOKAAL*

A *proeflokaal* is a bar where you drink *jenever*. Originally these places were attached to breweries. Inside you'll find a wide range of beers as well as spirits. Usually open from 11am-8pm.

De Ooievaar

Sint Olofspoort, 1 (corner of Zeedijk)
☎ 420 80 04
Open every day 1pm-1am.

The building housing this venerable institution tilts a little because of its age (1620) and not because you've drunk too many little frosted glasses of highly-flavoured *oud*. This *proeflokaal* dedicated to the stork is one of the oldest and nicest of them all.

De Admiraal

Herengracht, 319
☎ 625 43 34.

Rustic decor with barrels piled right up to the ceiling and wooden tables where you can try the *jenevers* made by van Wees, the oldest distillery in Jordaan. You can also enjoy a candlelit dinner here.

Het Proeflokaal

Pijlsteeg, 31 ☎ 622 53 34.

The old Wyn and Fockink distillery founded in 1679 has reopened in an alleyway behind the Dam. Here you can sample both its own products and other brands of liqueur and *jenever* in a very cosy atmosphere.

In de Wildeman

Kolksteeg, 3. ☎ 638 23 48.

A lovely place near the station and the red light district. The decor looks like an interior in a Dutch painting, with its copper chandeliers, wood panelling and black and white tiled floor. A choice of 150 types of beer, including 18 on draught.

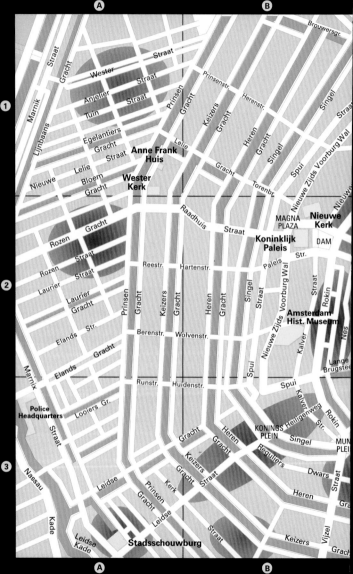

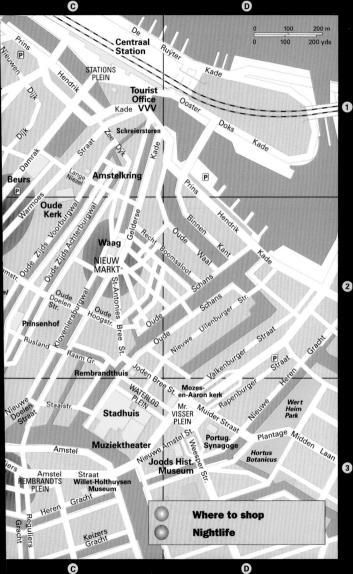

shopping Practicalities

(with antique shops on Nieuwe Spiegelstraat and Van Baerle and P.C. Hooft street). The big stores (De Bonneterie, Vroom & Dreesmann, Bijenkorf, Hema, etc.) are also open on Sunday afternoons. Lastly, remember that several markets are held on Sundays, including the ones specialising in contemporary art, bric-a-brac and secondhand goods, antiques and flowers (the flower market is only open in summer, though).

HOW TO PAY

Only buy from prosperous and respectable-looking dealers and beware of anything that might seem like a good bargain. If you're buying a work of art, you can ask for a certificate of authenticity, which the seller is obliged to provide. Generally speaking, you must ensure that you get a receipt for all your purchases. You may be asked to present it at customs and it may be

OPENING HOURS

In general, shop opening hours are 1-6pm on Mondays and 9/10am-6pm Tuesday to Friday. Most have late-night shopping on Thursdays till 9pm, but close earlier on Saturdays, at 5pm. Some branches of the food retail chain Albert Heijn stay open until 8 or 10pm.

WHERE CAN YOU SHOP ON SUNDAYS?

You'll find shops open in the city centre, on Kalverstraat, Damrak, Leidsestraat, and near the Noorderkerk,

particularly in Herenstraat. The current trend more or less all across the city is for shops to open from around 12/1-5pm on the first Sunday of the month during the summer season. This is also true of the commercial district around the Rijksmuseum

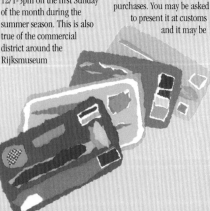

useful should you ever want to resell an item, or when completing your insurance claim if you suffer a burglary.

Most shops will accept payment by card, especially Visa, Mastercard and Eurocard, for purchases over 50Fl. For other cards, you should check the stickers on the shop door before you go inside. Eurocheques and traveller's cheques are accepted everywhere. In any case, it's always better value to withdraw cash in guilders directly from your own bank account using a cash machine than to pay for your purchase in a different currency.

FINDING YOUR WAY

Next to each address in the Shopping and Nightlife sections we have given its location on the map of Amsterdam on pages 80-81.

everywhere. The only traders exempt from this requirement are dealers in secondhand goods and antiques, so you can usually indulge in a bit of haggling when buying from them. But remember, Holland has a long and proud history as a trading nation, so don't expect to get away with reductions of more than 10 or 15% on the original price.

CUSTOMS FORMALITIES

There are no customs formalities when making purchases for EU citizens, provided they can show a receipt proving that duty on their purchase was paid in the Netherlands. There are no specific regulations in the case of antiques, as long as you can produce a certificate of authenticity and a bill made out by the seller.

HOW MUCH TO PAY

Traders are obliged by law to indicate the price of each item, so you won't get any nasty (or nice) surprises at the cash desk: there are labels

If you're caught in possession of forged documents, the goods will be confiscated and you'll have to pay a heavy fine. You may also be charged with receiving stolen goods when you get back home.

INTERNATIONAL TRANSPORTATION

If you want to send your new Malasian wood sofa home, or that pair of Delftware garden stools you've just treated yourself to, you have the choice of sending it by air, which is quick but expensive, or, if you are delivering it within Europe, by road, when how long it takes depends on how much you're prepared to pay. Insurance cover is almost always included in the transportation charge.

Here are some useful addresses in Amsterdam:

Büch B.V.
☎ 696 37 77.
Specialist in the transportation of works of art by road and air. They deliver worldwide.

Hendriks B.V.
☎ 587 81 23.
Road transport of all types of goods. They deliver all over Europe.

Charter
☎ 654 32 10.
Air freight transport. They deliver worldwide.

Those who aren't resident in the European Union may be able to get a reimbursement of VAT paid on larger purchases. by means of a rather complicated procedure. If you want to do this, ask the seller for a special form (*certificaat van uitvoer* OB90), which you'll then have to fill in at the border.

For more information, contact the Netherlands' customs service:
☎ 06 01 43 Freephone.

WOMEN'S FASHION

In the past women's fashion in Holland has tended to be comfortable and well-made, in natural fibres, rather than outrageously fashionable. However in recent years independent designers have developed original styles, some wild, some smart, but often at very affordable prices for unique items, while the bright colours and artificial fabrics used in Dutch off-the-peg fashions will add zest to any young woman's wardrobe.

Fever

Prinsengracht, 192 (A1)
☎ 623 45 00
Westerkerk
Trams 13, 14, 17
Open Wed.-Fri. noon-6pm,
Sat. 11am-5pm.

In her garage warehouse, with its floor decorated with painted marine motifs, Wilma Penning dresses all the elegant women who have a taste for adventure. Pride of place goes to silk and leather, with bright colours for every season. Here you'll find a light, transparent coat in pink silk, a closely tailored jacket and matching accessories (hats and gloves). A peach of a collection.

Oilily

Van Baerlestraat, 26 (not on map), ☎ 400 45 43
Mon. 1-6pm, Tue.-Sat.
9.30am-6pm, Thu. until
9pm, Sun. noon-5pm.

In this elegant, unfussy ambiance, with lovely wood-panelling on the walls, you'll find young, invigorating styles. Skirts, jumpers and blouson jackets in modern, brightly-coloured fabrics. This is the place to treat yourself to a pair of pink or yellow rubber boots to banish the grey from a rainy day. Jumpers from 249Fl. Blousons from 489Fl.

Timeless Collection

Prinsenstraat, 26 (B1)
☎ 638 17 60
Noordermarkt
Open Tue.-Sat. 11am-6pm.

The shop's decor is as elegant as the clothes in their sober colours. The Timeless collection favours silks and natural fibres such as wool, cotton and suede, depending on the season. Here you'll find smart suits, very simple evening dresses, swimsuits and a wide range of classic shirts and jackets. Nothing is very exciting, but every item is well-designed, sensible, wearable and made in lovely fabrics. A jacket will cost you around 400Fl

Liesbeth Royaards

Herengracht, 70
(near Herenstraat-B1)
☎ 626 50 26
Open Tue.-Sat. noon-6pm.

If you want to rediscover the atmosphere of the great couturiers of the 19th century, go up to the first floor of this beautiful old building where you may be greeted by Liesbeth Royaards, a designer for the last twenty years.

Her original creations are inspired as much by 17th-century dress as fifties fashions. She cleverly combines crinolines, silks, taffetas, tulle, shantung, wool and velvet, to create a diaphanous evening dress or a comfortable suit. Ensembles from between 1,400 and 2,000Fl, evening dresses from 3,000Fl. Everything's tailor-made, of course.

M/L Collections

Hartenstraat, 5 (B2)
☎ 620 12 16
Dam
Open Tue.-Fri. 11am-6pm, Thu. 10am-9pm, Sat. 10am-5pm.

The ultimate in Dutch off-the-peg fashions in a high-tech atmosphere of black and white. Here you'll find nothing that's truly eccentric. Instead the clothes are elegant and lovely to wear, made using natural and synthetic fibres. Prices are reasonable and, if you come during the sales, you can get some really fantastic bargains. Jacket 635Fl, blouse 115Fl and skirt 225Fl.

Henk Hendriks Couture

Herengracht, 360 (between Huidenst. and Leidsegracht-B3)
☎ 620 41 96
Open Tue.-Sat. 11am-5pm.

Designer Henk Hendriks opens his studio to women, and also sometimes to men, creating exclusive, made-to-measure clothes. Designs are made up first in cotton, after which you have to wait two weeks to be able to wear a unique item in the fabric and colour of your choice. Clothes can be sent anywhere in Europe. Expect to pay 3,000Fl for a man's suit and about 2,000Fl for a lady's suit or a dress.

Demask

Zeedijk 64 (C1)
☎ 620 56 03
Centraal Station
Mon.-Sat. 10am-7pm, Thu. until 9pm, Sun. noon-5pm.

Surprise yourself by visiting this highly specialised shop. For the more timid among you, Demask offers lingerie in lacquered leather, with chains and nails for the more extrovert. You can also find rubber mini-skirts, long latex gloves and some very saucy bodices. And that's before you go into the back room, where you'll find enough artefacts to awaken the demon within, even if you've got absolutely no imagination at all.

Cellarrich Connexion

Haarlemmerdijk, 98 (A1)
☎ 626 55 26
Open Mon. 1-6pm, Tue.-Fri. 10am-6pm, Sat. 10am-5pm.

It's the price of success – the four girls who started out selling leather goods in a cellar near Prinsengracht have had to move to a larger shop. They've kept to the same minimalism in the decor, though, to show off their creations to best effect. The bags and accessories have that amusing touch on which their reputation is based – real leather and fake crocodile skin, knitted leather pouches and trapezoid bags.

Vanilia

Van Baerlestraat, 30 (not on map), ☎ 672 32 08
Trams 2, 3, 5, 12
Open Tue.-Sat. 10am-6pm, Thu. until 9pm, Mon. 1-6pm, Sun. noon-5pm.

Fashions of the 1920s and 30s in colours and cuts to raise a few eyebrows. Lots of cotton, but also synthetic materials that are fluid and lovely to wear. The prices are pretty affordable considering that this is such a chic, expensive street. Dresses at 150Fl and jackets at 220Fl.

Hoeden M/V

Herengracht 422 (B3)
☎ 626 30 38
Leidsestraat
Trams 1, 2, 5, 11
Open Tue.-Fri. 10am-6pm, Thu. until 9pm, Sat. 10am-5pm, Mon. 1-6pm.

The great drawing-room of an old residence provides the showcase for this wonderful collection of hats created by Dutch, German and British designers. Here you'll find an enormous range, in all the colours and materials you can think of, from simple styles at 80Fl to sumptuous wide-brimmed straw hats at 800Fl. And on a practical note, the fitting service (reduction or enlargement) will give you the style you want in the size you want in under an hour.

Van Heek Lust for Leather

Brouwersgracht, 226b (not on map), ☎ 627 07 78
Thu. noon-9pm, Fri.-Sat. noon-6pm and by appt.

Joyce Van Heek herself both designs and makes her leather wear for men and women, including lingerie, waistcoats, trousers, demure skirts and others with daringly gaping laces at the back. Loads of designs and sizes

to choose from, but you can also have something made to measure. If you want to do this, have some documentation sent to you before you leave for Amsterdam. The use of very fine calfskin (instead of the usual lambskin) justifies the slightly higher prices (lace-up skirt, 395Fl).

De Petsalon

Hazenstraat, 3 (A3)
☎ **624 73 85**
Jordaan, Lauriergracht
Open Tue.-Sat. noon-6pm.

In a city where the bicycle is king it hardly comes as a surprise that there's a shop specialising in helmets made in all kinds of shapes and materials. For real class, you can't go further than a matching helmet and saddle! This very kitsch shop also offers crazy belts and sunglasses to add the finishing touches to your ultra-cool look.

Female & Partners

Spuistraat, 100
☎ **620 91 52**
Tue.-Sat. 11am-6pm,
Sun. and Mon. 1-6pm.

Amsterdam's top shop for erotic lingerie for women (and their partners) is not for the shy or faint-hearted. Esther and Ellen are pioneers in their field, offering an

entire range of contemporary erotic fashions. The Viva Maria, Undressed and Murray & Vern collections are the best in the genre. The huge tattoo sported by the young woman who receives you gives an indication of the kind of eccentricities you'll find inside.

Hester van Eeghen

Hartenstraat, 1 (B2)
☎ **626 92 12**
Dam
Open Mon. 1-6pm,
Tue.-Sat. 11am-6pm.

There's no two ways about it, this is where you must come if you want a truly original handbag. Round, square or triangular, they're all both amusing and functional. While the designs are Dutch, the lovely coloured materials are Italian, and they're made in Italy too. To complete the look, buy a matching wallet, key-ring, card-holder and diary in the same leather and colour.

Palette

Nieuwezijds Voorburgwal, 125
☎ **639 32 07**
Nieuwekerk (B2)
Open Mon., Wed. 1-6pm,
Tue., Thu., Fri. 11am-6pm,
Sat. 11am-5pm.

This miniature shop leaning its back against the Nieuwe Kerk specialises in making shoes in silks and satins. Even the most particular Cinderellas will find shoes to suit their feet here.

Indeed, with 500 shades on offer, how could you fail to find just the right shoes and accessories to match your little evening dress? (See p. 39)

Eva Damave

Tweede Laurierdwarsstraat, 51c (A3)
☎ **627 73 25**
Jordaan. Trams 13, 14, 17
Open Wed.-Fri. noon-6pm,
Sat. noon-5pm.

With extravagant little jumpers, woollen skirts and jackets, extraordinary colours and original designs, Eva is the queen of knitwear. More sophisticated shoppers will particularly like the wonderfully comfortable jumpers embroidered in silk. Spoil yourself, they're not that expensive (150-200Fl for a jumper).

(See p. 39)

Clothes & shoe sizes

Don't forget that on the continent shoe sizes and clothes sizes are different from what you may be used to, but the sales assistant should be able to help you find the perfect fit.

To help you navigate your way through the different sizes and choices we have included conversion tables on page 128. These list not only clothes and shoe sizes, but also weights and measurements.

MEN'S FASHION

For a long time now elegant Dutch men have been wearing Italian fashions, which are well represented in the chic shops of Van Baerlestraat and P.C. Hooftstraat. Dutch men's fashions aren't terribly inventive, with two exceptions – sportswear, which is well-made, practical and reasonably cheap, and the impeccably-cut leather wear.

Robin & Rik

Runstraat, 30 (A3)
☎ 627 89 24
Spui. Trams 1, 2, 5
Open Tue.-Sat. 11am-6pm,
Thu. until 9pm,
Mon. 1-6pm.

All you need to dress in leather from head to toe – trousers, jackets, tank tops, waistcoats and caps in different types of leather and skin. Those who like close-fitting clothes are well served here, particularly since Robin and Rik also do made-to-measure garments. Nothing you could really wear to a business meeting, but guaranteed to cause a stir if you're going to a gay club.

The Shirt Shop

Reguliersdwarstraat, 64 (B3)
☎ 423 20 88
Open Mon.-Sat. noon-7pm,
Sun. noon-6pm.

Don't try looking in this little shop if you're after a classic shirt. In here they're made of satin, velvet, or moiré, or patterned with spots or checks, in other words they're shirts for going out in, chatting up someone nice or just strutting your stuff. The brands are British, Dutch and sometimes Italian, all of them very exclusive and trendy. If you feel daring you could try the condom T-shirt. You won't spend more than 100Fl here, honest.

Stilett

Damstraat, 14 (B2)
☎ 625 28 54
Open every day 11am-6pm.

If you're sick of seeing everyone else wearing your T-shirt, usually shouting out the brand name of some American sportswear manufacturer, this is the shop for you. Stilett puts only exclusive and heavily-protected designs on its excellent quality polo shirts (that's

why we can't show you a photo!) From humour to provocation or quotation, here you'll find something you can be sure you'll never see elsewhere. From 25Fl.

Dockers

Leidsestraat, 11 (A3)
☎ 638 72 92
Trams 1, 2, 5, 11
Open Tue.-Sat. 9.30am-6pm,
Thu. until 9pm, Mon., Sun.
noon-6pm.

Levi's have created a new line of jeans, shirts, polo shirts and jackets under the name Dockers.

The wide range of colours and cuts maintains the comfort and quality on which the world-wide reputation of the brand is based. The usual American sizes.

Haberdashery

P.C. Hooftstraat, 53 (not on map)
☎ **672 01 89**
Trams 2, 3, 5, 12
Open Tue.-Fri. 10am-6pm, Thu. until 9pm, Sat. 10am-5pm, Mon. 1-6pm.

This shop specialises in made-to-measure suits for businessmen who lack imagination and is the only place in the Netherlands to sell this German brand. If you want to be clever you can have a second pair of trousers to match the jacket, while those with long arms or big necks can have their shirts altered accordingly. Anything is possible here and the prices aren't too wild (500-800Fl for a suit). Quality guaranteed.

Hoeden M/V

Herengracht, 422 (B3)
☎ **626 30 38**
Leidsest. Trams 1, 2, 5, 11
Open Tue.-Fri. 10am-6pm, Thu. until 9pm, Sat. 10am-5pm, Mon. 1-6pm.

Are you looking for a real panama hat or a Borsalino, or perhaps a cap or a boater? Then hurry to Marly Vroemen's shop, which specialises in hats for men and women. A Borsalino will set you back about 200Fl and the hat will be altered to fit your head in the twinkling of an eye.

CONTINENTAL SIZES

Men's shoe sizes are also different on the continent and clothes generally tend to be cut on the generous side. See the conversion tables on page 128 for more information.

Sissy-Boy

Van Baerlestraat, 12 (not on map) ☎ **672 02 47**
Kalverstraat, 199 (B2)
☎ **638 93 05**
Open Tue.-Sat. 9.30am-6pm, Thu. until 9pm, Mon. 1-6pm.

Don't be put off by the name. This is an excellent Dutch label for sporty, contemporary clothes aimed at 20-30 year-olds. They're not afraid to use colour here. The cuts tend to be fairly conventional, but you can find more amusing styles. The prices are in everyone's range: shirts at 99Fl at trousers at 150-200Fl.

Non Solo Blu

Herenstraat, 21 (B1)
☎ **639 09 12**
Spui. Trams 1, 2, 5
Open Mon.-Sat. 11am-6pm, Sun. Oct.-Jun.

Fashions for the trendy young man about Amsterdam. Exclusive Danish and British lines as well as items created here and made up in the little workshop next door. A very designer atmosphere, with fine cotton shirts, jumpers with rubber motifs, blouson jackets in synthetic sheepskin and also sometimes in cord. The clothes in their new lines reveal a flair for design and an understanding of what looks good. Expect to make a small investment, say around 200-500 florins.

FOR CHILDREN

In Amsterdam, they did away with layettes years ago. Here the by-word is imagination, with natural fibres, comfortable clothes and matching accessories. Classic, sporty, a touch of the hippy or truly ice-cool, your only problem is you're spoilt for choice. And to make your children's happiness complete, why not take them

Trix & Rees

Sint Antoniesbreestrat, 130
☎ **420 25 30**
Metro Nieuwmarkt (C2)
Open Tue.-Sat. 10am-6pm,
Thu. until 9pm,
Mon., Sun. 1-6pm.

Why shouldn't little ones be ultra-cool too? Sheepskin jackets, jumpers in chunky wool and T-shirts in natural cotton. Of course, everything is cut primarily for comfort – in other words the clothes are roomy. New-age mums will find everything for their children aged 0-8 here, as well as the 'adult' versions for themselves. Be prepared to pay 60Fl for a T-shirt and 100Fl for a little dress.

Oilily Store

P.C. Hooftstraat, 131-133
(not on map)
☎ **672 33 61**
Trams 2, 3, 5, 12 .
Open Tue.-Fri. 10am-6pm,
Thu. until 9pm, Sat. 10am-
5pm, Mon. 1-6pm, Sun.
noon- 6pm.

If you've had enough of lavender blue and pastel pink, Oilily is the line of imaginative, colourful clothes

you've been looking for. Here you'll find little flowers, hearts, butterflies and checks on the accessories too (bags, shoes, socks, wooden jewellery and hair clips). Of course, you have to pay for it (embroidered T-shirt 100Fl, ensemble 200Fl).

Boon & Co

Gravenstraat, 11 (B1)
☎ **620 84 38**
Nieuwekerk
Open Wed.-Fri. 11am-6pm,
Sat. 11am-5pm.

Lovely little ensembles for babies (0-2 years), designed by Frédérique de Tombe. To prevent allergies, the fabrics (wool and cotton) are 100% natural. Two collections a year at average prices (ensembles at 90Fl, jumpers at 50Fl and shoes at 150Fl).

't Klompenhuisje

Nieuwe Hoogstraat, 9a (C2)
☎ 622 81 00
Metro Nieuwmarkt
Open Mon.-Sat. 10am-6pm.

This company started out as a specialist producer of clogs for children, but has since expanded its production to other kinds of shoe, including sandals, walking boots and smart shoes. Expect to pay between 30Fl for a pair of clogs and 100Fl for more complicated types of shoe. A prettily-decorated shop which is a real paradise of children's footwear.

Teuntje

Haarlemmerdijk, 71 (not on map)
Jordaan ☎ 625 34 32
Open Mon.-Fri. 10am-6pm,
Sat. 10am-5pm.

Danish, Belgian and Dutch brands you can't find anywhere else, with clothes in cotton and other comfortable fabrics. Browns, dark greens and black are common in these extremely well-cut clothes at good prices (from 12Fl).

De Speelmuis

Elandsgracht, 58 (A2)
☎ 638 53 42
Mon. 1-6pm, Tue.-Fri. 10am-6pm, Sat. 10am-5pm.

Who could resist these exquisite dolls' houses full of charming details that take us back to childhood? Suddenly we're changed into Gullivers in Lilliput, transported to a fairy-tale world filled with miniature sofas, vases, flowers and tables, where adults just seem too big. Some fragile, expensive items are really the preserve of collectors and dolls house-lovers rather than little children. House prices start at 99Fl each. There's also a fine range of wooden toys and spinning tops. It's a paradise for children large and small.

De Kinderbrillenwinkel

Nieuwezijdsvoorburgwal, 131 (B2) ☎ 626 40 91
Tue.-Fri. 11am-6pm, Sat. 11am-5pm, Mon. by appt.

This amusing shop specialises in glasses for children. You'll find a frame to suit every taste – green, yellow or blue, round or oval and always different. But if your children are unpersuadably vain and you happen to have their prescription handy, you'll find here safe, comfortable contact lenses specially adapted for their eyes. There's also a wide range of very amusing old frames available from 150Fl a pair. You can easily have the correct lenses fitted when you get home.

Belltree

Spiegelgracht, 10 (B3)
☎ 625 88 30
Rijksmuseum. Trams 6, 7, 10
Open Tue.-Sat. 10am-6pm.

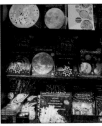

You'll find here wonderful dolls' tea-sets with Delftware decorations, amazing musical boxes, kaleidoscopes , mechanical toys and roundabouts, not to mention educational toys to teach your children all about our planet, in other words, wonderful toys for children of all ages from 10Fl.

> ### CHILDREN'S CLOTHES SIZES
>
> As with adult clothes, the cut of your children's clothes tends to be quite generous.
> 0-1 year: 56/74cm (22/29in);
> 1-3 years: 80/98cm (32/39in);
> 3-8 years: 104/176cm (40/69in).

FLOWERS AND GARDENS

Amsterdammers are true worshippers of flowers and plants, which they use to decorate their homes, balconies and little gardens. It's hard not to be caught up by this passion when you walk past the stalls in the flower market, particularly since the prices are so low and there's such a wealth of choice, especially for plants grown from bulbs. The garden furniture and earthenware pots are also very tempting.

Riviera

Herenstraat, 2-6 (B1)
☎ 622 76 75
Noordermarkt
Open Mon.-Fri. 9am-6pm, Sat. 9am-5pm, Sun. noon-5pm.

Here you'll find loads of ideas for decorating your garden, as well as the prettiest floral arrangements in town. Lights with reflectors, wrought-iron lamps (50Fl), scented candles, cane armchairs, bronze bowls and teak garden furniture, not to mention engraved crystal glasses. If you really can't resist a superb teak bench (450-1,200Fl) or a lounger (600Fl), they can be sent back home for you. The best place in Amsterdam for all you garden-lovers.

Vivaria

Ceintuurbaan, 5 (not on map)
☎ 676 46 06
Open Tue.-Fri. 10am-6pm, Sat. until 5pm.

This amazing shop sells nothing but terrariums, little indoor greenhouses in which you can easily grow ferns, lichens, mosses and wild orchids that will remind you of the primeval forest where all life began, including our own. These tiny decorative gardens are housed inside panes of glass set into frames of different shapes and sizes and will more or less look after themselves, as long as you make sure they have water and light. It's like having an aquarium without fish, just as decorative and much less of a hassle.

Hiernaast

Herenstraat, 30 (B1)
☎ 623 36 67
Noordermarkt
Open Mon.-Fri. 11am-6pm, Sat. 11am-5pm.

Here you'll find earthenware pots that will remind you of Tuscany, Medici vases, lovely coloured glasses, glazed ceramics, lamps with reflectors, lanterns of all kinds, old and new, all piled up more or less everywhere, on shelves and all over the floor. The stock varies according to availability and the time of year. The big decorative jugs and vases will give your patio or terrace a flavour of Provence or Italy. Reflecting lamps at 20Fl, coloured glasses 6Fl each.

Outras Coisas

Herenstraat, 31 (B1)
☎ 625 72 81
Noordermarkt
Open Mon. 11am-6.30pm, Tue.-Fri. 10am-6.30pm, Sat. 5.30pm.

Crockery and garden furniture that's so beautiful and simple

you'd be happy to use it inside as well. Pretty cotton tablecloths, enamelled dishes with matching napkins, stoneware crockery, picnic hampers and large candles in unusual shapes. The lovely Dutch-made iron tables are 275Fl each. Lots of decorative ideas for

your patio or balcony, and for your living-room too.

Flower market

Amstelveld
Prinsengracht. Tram 4.

Less well-known than the floating market of Singel, this is a charming flower market which is held on Monday mornings on the shady Amstelveld square, near a wooden church. Stalls stacked with cut flowers rub shoulders with others selling indoor or garden plants.

Kees Bevaart

Singel (opposite 508-B3)
☎ 625 82 82
Muntplein
Trams 4, 9, 14, 16, 24, 25
Open Mon.-Sat. 8.30am-5.30pm,also Sun. in summer.

Of all the stalls in the floating market, this one is the best stocked with hardy and seasonal plants. Here you'll find plant varieties you may never have seen before, as well as good advice on how to grow them.

De Tuin

Singel (opposite 502-B3)
☎ 625 45 71
Muntplein
Trams 4, 9, 14, 16, 24, 25
Open Mon.-Sat. 8am-5pm
and also Sunday in summer.

This is *the* place to buy tulips. You'll find a very extensive range, including the famous black tulip 'Queen of Night'. There are also 500 varieties of bulbs, such as narcissus, daffodils, dahlias, hyacinths, freesias, lilies, begonias and amaryllis. Ignoramuses can have everything explained to them in English. It'll cost you 6.50Fl for ten tulip bulbs.

BULB PRACTICALITIES

Bulbs for planting are sold from June to the end of December. If the winter has been hard, bulbs won't be available before the end of June at the earliest. Bulbs planted in the autumn will flower in spring, whereas those planted in spring (such as begonias, lilies and dahlias) will flower in autumn. If you have a heavy, clay soil, lighten it with sand and peat. See also p.19 on growing tulips.

Stins

Singel and Muntplein (B3)
☎ 625 72 22
Open Mon.-Sat. 9am-6pm
and also Sunday in summer.
Under a kind of arbour of bouquets of dried flowers, you'll find the loveliest flower arrangements in the market. Reasonable prices and a very extensive choice.

JEWELLERY AND ETHNIC GOODS

As well as the diamond trade, solidly established in Amsterdam since the 17th century, there are a number of shops and galleries specialising in ethnic artefacts. From magnificent jewellery in silver and coral to masks from Africa and the Pacific and traditional earthenware crockery, each deals in a particular category or part of the world.

jeweller's displaying diamonds and other precious stones set in gold or silver to suit every purse. A good place to get an idea of prices and to watch the different stages the stones pass through before being mounted.

Za-Za Diamonds

**Weteringschans, 89 (not on map), ☎ 626 27 98
Rijksmuseum. Trams 6, 7, 10
Open every day 9.30am-5.30pm.**

Watch the craftsmen at work in this diamond-cutting shop and you'll get a better idea of what makes these precious gems so expensive. This is also a renowned

Out of Africa

**Herengracht, 215 (and Raadhuisstraat-B2)
☎ 623 46 77
Trams 13, 14, 17
Open Mon. 10am-6pm, Tue., Thu. and Sat. 10am-5pm, Wed. and Fri. 11am-6pm, in summer Sun. noon-6pm.**

This fan of Queen Beatrix imports high-quality newly-made artefacts from west Africa and Zimbabwe. Among his treasures you'll find some beautiful necklaces with floral designs in glass (135Fl), printed cotton cloths from Ghana, Burkina Faso and Mali (from 150Fl), little cars and aeroplanes cut out from aluminium food cans (95Fl) and masks from Gabon.

Baobab

**Elandsgracht, 128 (A2)
Trams 7, 10
☎ 626 83 98
Open Mon.-Sat. 11am-6pm.**

A real Ali Baba's cave where, if you're prepared to search patiently, you'll find something rare and precious. Among the Buddhas, objects and cloth from Asia, and even some pre-Columbian pottery, you'll find an enormous choice of ethnic silver jewellery. All is of excellent quality, whether Indian, Turkoman, Yemeni, Ethiopian or Tibetan, and the prices are often affordable. Take your time and explore at your own pace. It would be surprising if you didn't find some original and exotic gift.

Kashba

**Staalstraat, 3 (C3)
☎ 623 55 64. Muntplein
Open Mon.-Sat. 11am-6pm.**

This pretty shop contains the finds gathered on the course of his journeys by an indefatigable

KASHBA

traveller who spends his time wandering the steppes of central Asia and the Indian subcontinent.

Here you'll find furniture from Rajasthan and southern India, including carved doors and lintels, as well as ikate cloth and many items of jewellery combining silver, turquoise, coral and lapis-lazuli. The high quality of these objects is reflected in the prices.

Gallery Steimer

Reestraat, 25 (A2)
☎ 624 42 20
Dam
Open Tue.-Fri. 11am-6pm,
Sat. 11am-5pm.

This artisan jewellery-maker creates classic, timeless pieces full of invention. He also draws the majority of his ideas from the past. If you'd like to wear jewels that will make you look like Nefertiti or a bracelet to make you feel like a Celtic princess or Roman matron, then Klaus Steimer will fulfil all your desires. By cleverly combining gold, silver and semi-precious stones, he produces

jewellery in antique styles, which he interprets with intelligence to give them a contemporary resonance. You can also have the piece of your choice made to order.

Bonebakker & Zoon

Rokin, 88-90 (B2)
☎ 623 22 94
Trams 4, 9, 14, 16, 24, 25
Open Mon.-Fri. 10am-
5.30pm, Sun. noon-4pm.

If you're looking for fun pieces, you won't find them here. The products sold by this supplier of jewellery to kings and princes since 1792 are strictly top of the range. It's worth having a look at the window display, though, even if you haven't the slightest intention of turning yourself into a Christmas tree. Although the diamonds are no longer cut on the premises, they're mounted in superb pieces, as are other precious stones. Certificates are provided for all items (the gold is 18 carats). Reception, quality and price to match, in other words royal.

De rare Kiek

(see p. 59)
Prinsengracht, 539 (A3).

An essential address for collectors of African art.

(see p. 59)

JEWELLERY PRACTICALITIES

In Holland every piece of gold or silver jewellery is stamped with an authenticating mark awarded by Gouda. This varies according to the number of carats (for 18 carat gold it's a tulip). In the case of ethnic jewellery on the other hand, there are no marks guaranteeing the silver content or the authenticity of the amber. A word of advice: amber is very rare and expensive. It has electrostatic qualities and gives off a slight scent when rubbed, for example, if the beads in a necklace rub against each other.

SOMETHING A LITTLE DIFFERENT

In this city that's so like a village, you have to try to stand out from your neighbours. Recent times have seen the opening of a great many amusing shops specialising in surprising and downright bizarre objects. Most of these are in Jordaan and beyond Prinsengracht. Now it's your turn to explore them.

Christmas Palace
Singel, 508 (B3)
☎ **421 01 55**
Every day 9am-6pm.

Beat the end-of-year rush by calmly choosing your Christmas decorations here. Angels, garlands, gilded candles, paper napkins decorated with stars, Christmas trees, Father Christmases and even a special edition of Delftware for your Christmas dinner, in other words everything you need to prepare for the festive season to the sound of carols and Christmas songs, all year round.

Von & Vic
Herenstraat, 37 (B1)
☎ **639 17 07**
Mon., Wed.-Fri. 11am- 6pm, Sat. 5.30pm, Sun. noon-5pm.

They change colour according to your mood, or have solar cells or play music; some are retro, others weird and they even tell the right time. The *Fossil* watch comes in

300 versions, from 100-160Fl. The *Greenpeace* watch runs on solar energy, or choose one with hands to match your profession (*Akteo*, 185Fl).

Titus Crynen
Bethanienstraat, 2 (C2)
☎ **623 94 39**
and ☻ 623 98 51,
by appointment.

Gustav Leonhardt, Frans Brüggen, Ton Koopman, there are plenty of 'Baroque' musicians in the Netherlands because of the conservatoire in The Hague, which is one of the most famous in Europe for music of the period. It's hardly surprising that lovers of 17th and 18th-century music love Amsterdam. Titus Crynen is known as a restorer and maker of harpsichords copied from old instruments. This would be a truly magnificent gift to yourself. You choose the decoration on the case and the instrument can be delivered to your home and tuned there. It will cost between 24,000 and 40,000Fl, though.

Knopenwinkel
Wolvenstraat, 14 (B2)
☎ **624 04 79**
Spui. Trams 1, 2, 5,
Tue.-Sat. 11am-6pm,
Mon. 1-6pm.

The walls of this shop are literally covered with buttons. You can't

fail to find the one you need or one to inspire your dressmaking. For 10 years Dorothea de Boer has been collecting thousands of

buttons of all shapes and materials except plastic. They'll give even the least imaginative dress-maker some ideas.

De Witte Tandenwinkel
Runstraat, 5 (A3)
☎ **623 34 43**
Mon. 1-6pm, Tue-Fri. 10am-6pm, Sat. 10am-5pm

A colourful treat for your jaws! This is the toothbrush palace. Fluorescent , Mickey Mouse-shaped, electric, designer – you'll find them all here, along with the most sophisticated toothpaste and most amazing tooth mugs. Everything to liven up your daily brushing and great ideas for amusing, inexpensive little gifts. From 10Fl.

't Mannetje in Transport

Quellijnstraat, 48 (not on map)
☎ **679 21 39**
Mon.-Fri. 9am-6pm,
Sat. 9am-5pm.

Don't leave Amsterdam without at least considering buying a bicycle. This is a shop all pedal-pushing enthusiasts will love. A very wide range of unusual and made-to-measure bikes, adapted to suit your needs. Ideal for shopping in town or exploring the flat countryside, and perfect for showing off at home with a machine like nobody else's. Prices start at 1,300Fl. Their most popular bike has a carrier attached with seats for up to 6 (small!) children which you can also hire for the day.

Funframes Decoration

Tweede Egelantiersdwarsstraat, 16 (A1)
☎ **639 39 02**
Jordaan, Westerkerk
Tue.-Fri. 11am-6pm,
Sat. 10am-5pm.

A tiny shop specialising in ornate and unusual frames has just opened in the heart of Jordaan. From smallest (2x3cm/ ¾x1in) to largest (20x30cm/8x12in), most Zen to most wild, you can't accuse the designers from Holland and elsewhere of lacking imagination.

Frames of driftwood, hand-painted wood, metal, decorated with angels or shells, 5-200Fl each.

Nieuws

Prinsengracht, 297 (A1)
☎ **627 95 40**
Open Tue.-Fri. 10am-6.30pm, Thu. 9pm.

It's hard to say whether this shop is gadget heaven or the future space lab the kids are so keen on. An essential stop for novelty-lovers, this is the place for edible underwear, ready-faded flowers,

shampoo for bald men, fake goldfish that look more real than the real ones, in other words anything and everything you can't get elsewhere.Proves you don't need a rocket to be a space-cadet.

SEE ALSO:

Condomerie Het Gulden Vlies , Warmoesstraat, 141.
☎ 627 41 74 (see p. 47).
Every kind of condom.

Coppenhagen, 1001 kralen, Rozengracht, 54.
☎ 624 36 81 (see p. 51).
Hundreds of glass beads for you to make your own jewellery.

INTERIOR DESIGN

Gerrit Rietveld, one of the major exponents of the *de Stijl* movement, became famous with his zig-zag chair, which could be easily mass-produced. Today's Dutch designers are just as creative, producing imaginative designs for furniture and lighting. Japanese furniture and exotic accessories match their strict, simple shapes to perfection.

Avenue 110

Singel, 110 (B2)
☎ 627 96 65
Noordermarkt
Open Tue.-Fri. 10am-6pm, Sat. noon-5pm.

An essential stop for Japanese, Korean and Chinese furniture at good prices. In tune with such foreign pieces, you'll also find here the giants of Art Deco and modernism – Hoffmann, Mies van der Rohe, Le Corbusier, Rietveld and Mackintosh. Beautiful old carpets and hand-painted lamps by Corine van Der Werf.

Fanous Ramadan

Runstraat, 33 (A3)
☎ 423 23 50
Mon. 1-6pm, Tue.-Sat. 11am-6pm, Sun. 1-5pm.

A *fanous ramadan* is an Egyptian lamp lit on the very last evening of the Ramadan period. This little shop on the corner of Runstraat and Prinsengracht specialises in every kind of oriental lamp, including lamps made of glass, metal and copper. This is also where you'll find the rarest pieces to recreate the soft light of the thousand-and-one nights.

The Frozen Fountain

Prinsengracht, 629 (B1)
☎ 622 93 75
Tue.-Fri. 10am-6pm, Mon. 1-6pm, Sat. 10am-5pm.

A new exhibition is held every month in this gallery-shop showcasing the latest creations by talented young Dutch designers. From decorative items to made-to-measure furniture, you'll always find plenty of ideas and often gifts to take home with you.

Prices vary greatly, from 10 to 10,000Fl. A hairdresser and stylist moved in recently, so you can make practical use of your time spent contemplating all these beautiful objects. A superb shop absolutely not to be missed.

Koot

Raadhuisstraat, 55 (B2)
☎ 626 48 30
Trams 13, 14, 17
Open Mon. 1-6pm, Tue.-Fri. 9am-6pm Thu. until 9pm, Sat. 10am-5pm.

The new art of living Dutch-style, interpreted in lamps and objects created by great designers, including the fashionable Jan Des Bouvrie, Rob Eekhardt, Maroeska Metz and Anet van Egmond.

Maranòn

Singel, 488-490 (B2)
☎ 622 59 38
Trams 4, 9, 14, 16, 24, 25
Open Mon.-Sat. noon-6pm, Sun. 10am-5pm.

With this range of 150 hammocks from South America, there's no way you could fail to find one you'd just love to hang in. Indoor hammocks in cotton and sisal, outdoor hammocks in hemp,

in varying sizes, from 3m/4ft to 6m/8ft, and weights, from light to heavy canvas, for one or two people. Prices range from 75Fl for a net hammock to 2,000Fl for a hand-embroidered hammock.

Klamboe Imports

Prinsengracht, 232 (A2)
☎ **622 94 92**
Jordaan, Lauriergracht
Open Tue.-Fri. 11am-6pm.

In the heat of midsummer who hasn't dreamed of a light net floating round the bed to keep the mosquitoes at bay? Here you'll find every imaginable kind of mosquito net or *klamboe*. They come on round or rectangular frames and are made of nylon, light cotton or polyester. Prices from 65 to 95Fl for large mosquito nets, 49Fl for a traveller's net.

Jan Best

Keizersgracht, 357
(corner of
Huidenstraat-A3)
☎ **623 27 36**
Spui. Trams 1, 2, 5
Open Mon.-Fri. 10.30am-6pm, Sat. 10am-5pm.

If you can't buy yourself the original of one of these Art Deco lamps, here you'll find excellent reproductions which will also look very impressive in your home. Prices range from 95 to 2,000Fl depending on the type. The 20s-style metal wall-lamp costs 95Fl.

Gallery K.I.S

Paleisstraat, 107 (B2)
☎ **620 97 60**
Dam
Open Wed.-Sun. noon.-6pm

Kunst In Serie, or art in series, is a 200m²/2,000sqft exhibition of creations by the best designers from Holland and elsewhere. Furniture for the home or office,

If you just can't resist an item of furniture that's rather too cumbersome to take home with you, then go to a local carrier or Danzas, who will deliver your piece in between 1 and 4 days (see addresses on p. 81). Standards for lighting are the same in Holland as in the UK. Items may need adapting for use in other countries.

lighting, carpets and decorative objects that reflect new trends in design. It's goodbye to things made of plastic and hello to exotic woods, chrome, glass and wrought iron.

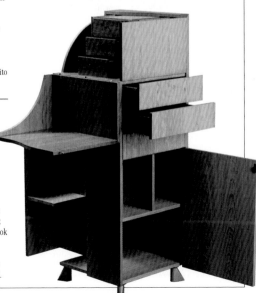

EXPLORING THE MARKETS

The way to a city's character is through its markets. Among their stalls, from the environmentally-friendly to the ever-so-slightly intellectual, you'll discover the true nature of Amsterdam. Best of all are the flower markets and flea markets, where you will find everything in a very cosmopolitan atmosphere.

Flower market

Singel (B2)
Every day in summer, 8am-5.30pm, winter closed Sun.

There's no way you could miss this market, which is very central and colourful all year round.

Flea market

Waterlooplein (C3)
Metro Waterlooplein
Mon.-Sat. 10am-5pm

Amsterdam's biggest flea market specialises in secondhand clothes. Depending on your imagination and dressmaking skills, they say you can dress yourself for next to nothing. Besides, as any designer

will tell you, they get their ideas from the flea market. As well as clothes, you'll find shoes, books, CDs and records, old postcards and army surplus. A special mention goes to the stalls selling Indonesian cloth and Indian jewellery, some of which is very beautiful and hard to find elsewhere. The same can't be said of the dealers and pickpockets, who you also need to watch out for. More pleasant discoveries can be made at the Waterloo Ware House a stone's throw away.

Stamp market (Postzegelsmarkt)

Nieuwezijds Voorburgwal (B2)
Spui. Wed. and Sat. 1-6pm.

A market for stamps and old coins is held twice a week opposite the Amsterdams Historisch Museum. Philatelists and coin collectors are bound to find something here to add to their collections. Business is conducted in a very professional atmosphere.

Secondhand book market

Oudeman Huispoort (B3)
Muntplein
Mon.-Sat. 11am-5pm.

In a delightfully picturesque 18th-century passage between Kloveniersburgwal and Oudezijds Voorburgwal, you'll find stalls selling books for collectors as well as old engravings. Take the time to explore. The Dutch are very good linguists and you're bound to find books in many languages, including plenty in English. You might also find original engravings or facsimile reproductions of 17th, 18th and 19th-century Amsterdam landscapes. All in all, lots of interesting souvenirs that won't be hard to carry home.

Art market (Kunstmarkt)

Spui (B3). Trams 1, 2, 5, 11
Sun. 9am-6pm, Mar.-early Dec.

You'll find good and bad in this market, where contemporary

artists regularly come to sell their work, which includes raku pottery, watercolours, sculpture and oil paintings. One excellent engraver, Wim van der Meij, sells originals from 65Fl each. Where paintings are concerned, it's all a matter of taste, but what you see here often compares very favourably with accredited galleries showing contemporary art.

Book market (Boekenmarkt)

Spui (B3). Trams 1, 2, 5, 11
Fri. 10am-6pm.

Poets read out their verses to a highly distinguished background accompaniment of notes played on a harp, while lovers of old books and collectors of rare ones rifle through the piles of old leather-bound volumes looking for special editions. A fascinating market, and one that's very typical of Amsterdam.

Bird and farm produce market

Noordermarkt (Sat. 9am-2pm) and Lindengracht (Sat. 9am-4pm) (A1)
Jordaan.

A lovely market, where ordinary Amsterdammers shop. Among the stalls of farm produce you'll find chicks and homing pigeons, as well as exotic birds. It is very popular with the inhabitants of Jordaan, who go to the cafés in the square when they've finished doing their shopping. On Monday mornings there is

a colourful secondhand market on Noordermarkt.

Albert Cuypmarkt general market

A. Cuypstraat (not on map)
Trams 4, 16, 24, 25
Mon.-Sat. 9am-5pm.

The busiest and most popular of the city's markets. A truly cosmopolitan crowd rub shoulders among the stalls selling fish, poultry, fruit and vegetables, spices, cheeses, cheap clothes, pots and pans and leather goods.

Bric-a-brac market

Nieuwmarkt (C2)
Metro Nieuwmarkt
Sun. 10am
to 5pm

A very disparate collection of items, from household objects to worn-out books and furniture on the verge of collapse. In other words, the ideal place to go rummaging if you like that kind of thing. There's loads of choice, but you wouldn't want to be in a hurry. There are a few new items if you get there early, particularly silverware, ceramics and glass, though ultimately it's not that cheap.

WATERLOO WARE HOUSE

Jodenbreestraat, 144 (C2)
Mon.-Sat. 9am-5pm, Sun.
11am-5pm.

From unusual objects to old ice-skates, this warehouse contains a thousand treasures at bric-a-brac prices. There's something here from every corner of the world – you'll find great big jugs and masks from Africa, but you might equally well come across an old piece of Delftware or an oriental carpet that's not too threadbare.

TABLEWARE AND FABRICS

Rare, beautiful and amusing objects from all over the world, particularly Asia, and fabrics in brilliant colours, for simple – or sumptuous – decorations for your home and table. Amsterdam has many shops selling fabrics you won't find easily elsewhere. But for a few years now high-tech decoration has been all the rage in Jordaan's shops, which keep a close eye on new fashion trends.

Kitsch Kitchen

Eerste Bloemdwarsstraat, 21 (A2)
☎ 428 49 09
Mon.-Fri. 11am-5.30pm, Sat. 10am-5pm.
Kitsch Kitchen Kids
Rozengracht, 183 (A2)
☎ 622 82 64
Mon.-Sat. 10.30am-6pm.

There's no need to go Mexico for funny, brightly-coloured, kitsch and very plastic household equipment,there's loads of it here. Fluorescent brooms, violet ladles, flowery waxed table-cloths and shopping bags, tequila glasses (5Fl), *papel picado* for the Mexican Day of the Dead and amulets of the Virgin Mary from Guadeloupe.

Terra

Reestraat, 21 (A2)
☎ 638 59 13
Tue.-Sat. 11am-6pm.

This little shop specialising in dishes and traditional pottery from Andalusia, has some wonderful faience and earthenware crockery with Moorish influences. Lots of them are modern, but there's also a small section selling real collector's items. How to make your table more interesting without spending a fortune.

Binnenhuis

Huidenstraat, 3-5 (B3)
☎ 622 15 84
Spui. Trams 1, 2, 5
Open Mon. 1-6pm, Tue.-Fri. 10am-6pm, Sat. 11am-5pm

Simply the best! A pioneer among shops selling contemporary and high-tech decorative items, whose products and new lines are regularly presented in Dutch home style magazines. Metal shelves that make waves across the walls, tulip-shaped wall-lamps and some really wild crockery, but also beautiful sheets with old-fashioned embroidery (695Fl). It isn't cheap, of course, but why not go and have a look anyway?

Hot Shop

Nieuwe Hoogstraat, 24 (C2)
☎ 625 58 50
Metro Nieuwmarkt
Open Mon. 1-6pm, Tue.-Fri. 10am-6pm, Sat. 10am-5pm.

The tone is set by a raw cotton throw on an azulejo tile table, with sun-drenched fabrics and earthenware, openwork braziers, old glasses and crescent moons in painted stucco, all from Spain and Portugal. If you want to redo your kitchen in white faience with blue decorations, you'll find azulejo tiles sold individually. Faience tiles are 5Fl each and the fabrics are 2.8m/3yds wide. At these prices, why deprive yourself?

Colorique

Huidenstraat, 30 (B3)
☎ 626 16 32
Spui. Trams 1, 2, 5
Open Mon.-Sat. 11am-6pm.

A kitsch, colourful little shop, piled high with Indian and Latin-American fabrics, wrought iron and small items of furniture. There are ikate and moiré fabrics, others with pleats or embroidery. They come in the form of bedspreads (175Fl), tablecloths (25-50Fl) and scarves. Loads of ideas to brighten up your kitchen, dining-room or bedroom.

Mc Lennan's

Hartenstraat, 22 (B2)
☎ 622 76 93
Dam
Open Mon. 1-6pm,
Tue.-Fri. 10.30am-6pm, Sat. 10.30am-5.30pm.

Step into the enticing world of the finest silks selected in the workshops of China, Thailand

and Vietnam. You'll find them stretched across the walls or raised like colourful banners. Raw, smooth, goffered, brocaded, satiny, printed and plain, this is where the Dutch couturiers come to stock up with crepe de Chine, shantung, taffeta and silk brocade. Expect to pay 49Fl to 59Fl a metre/39in for satin or crepe. Magnificent materials and colours.

Studio Bazar

Reguliersdwarsstraat, 60-62 (B3)
☎ 622 08 30
Muntplein
Open Mon. 1-6pm, Tue.-Fri. 10am-6pm, Thu until 9pm, Sat. 10am-5pm.

Despite the rather off-putting 'warehouse' concept, this is where you'll find the best lines in crockery, table linens and kitchen utensils with a contemporary feel. Frosted plastic 'Screwpull' corkscrews in ten colours (60Fl), Mickey Mouse kettles, flexible non-stick cake-moulds (67Fl), cactus fruit-squeezers and smart wicker picnic hampers: a real classic for Sundays in the

country that will never go out of style!

Capsicum

(see p. 44)
Oude Hoogstraat, 1 (B2).

Oriental linens, cotton and silk.

ANTIQUES AND CERAMICS

All the collectors know about Nieuwe Spiegelstraat, where you'll find Amsterdam's finest antique shops. But alongside these prestigious dealers, there are other, less well-known places where there are real bargains to be had, particularly fine pieces of old and new Delftware, which you could never find elsewhere. Engraved or sculpted glass is also part of the decor of traditional Dutch interiors.

Hogendoorn & Kaufman

Rokin, 124 (B3)
☎ 638 27 36
Trams 4, 9, 14, 16, 24, 25
Mon.-Sat. 10am-7pm,
Sun. 1-6pm.

The best address in town for buying modern Delft or Makkum ware. Pieces are selected in the two royal factories and are hand decorated by the best craftsmen. Everything from lovely Delft tiles 13x13cm/5x5in to elegant tulip vases, but you have to be prepared to spend some money – 50Fl for a decorated tile, 300Fl for a vase. The shop will have it sent home for you.

Holland Gallery De Munt

Muntplein, 12 (B3)
☎ 623 22 71
Open Mon.-Sat. 10am-6pm.

Make no mistake, this isn't a souvenir shop. On the contrary, it's a specialist outlet for fine Dutch faience. All the pieces sold here are signed, and all are made in one or other of the royal factories: 'Porceleyne Fles', Delft,

'Tichelaar' and Makkum. Faience tiles from 30Fl. A very wide choice.

Eduard Kramer

Nieuwe Spiegelstraat, 64 (B3)
☎ 627 41 52
Rijksmuseum
Trams 6, 7, 10
Open Thu.-Sat. noon-6pm.

In this antique shop, which specialises in old Delft and Makkum pieces, you have to pick your way with cat-like caution among the unbelievable piles of faience porcelain, glass and earthenware pipes. This is where you'll find the widest choice of glazed tiles. A little expensive if you want a complete makeover for your kitchen or bathroom, but there's nothing to stop you using one of these tiles as a table mat.

Peter Korf De Gidts

Nieuwe Spiegelstraat, 28 (B3)
☎ 625 26 25
Rijksmuseum
Trams 6, 7, 10
Open Tue.-Sat. 11am-6pm.

In the 18th century it was usual to give the gift of an engraved glass as a fragile souvenir of a religious or other family celebration. Fairly rare today, they're decorated with coats of arms, maxims, figures and landscapes. One of these would make a lovely, typically Dutch gift.

Van Glas

Ruysdaelstraat, 33 (not on map)
☎ 675 86 34
**Roelof Hartplein. Trams 3, 5, 12
Open Tue.-Fri. 11am-6pm,
Sat. 11am-5pm.**

Edwin Dieperink continues the tradition of the master glassworker with his blown glass, which he frosts and colours to make superb creations, from sculpture-carafes to decorative glasses, lamps and boxes. Visit the shop and see the amazing diversity of shapes that can be made from this magical material.

Steensma & Van der Plas

Prinsengracht, 272 (A2)
☎ 627 21 97
**Jordaan, Lauriergracht
Open Thu. and Fri.
11am-6pm, Sat. 11am-5pm
or by appt.**

These pieces of office and shop furniture and accessories, designed from 1880-1920, are beautiful, simple and functional. A display of exceptional pieces, from large clocks to wardrobes with sliding backs, in a beautiful space. Go and see.

Smokiana

(see p. 21).
Prinsengracht, 488
☎ 421 17 79

**Leidseplein. Trams 1, 2, 5, 11
Open Wed.-Sat.
noon-6pm.**

In this beautiful house by the canal you'll find a superb collection of pipes old and new, hookahs and tobacco pouches, as well as cigar, opium and betel

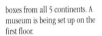

boxes from all 5 continents. A museum is being set up on the first floor.

Frans Leidelmeijer

(see p. 58 – B3)
Nieuwe Spiegelstraat, 58.

Specialises in Dutch Art Nouveau and Art Deco.

H.C. van Vliet

Nieuwe Spiegelstraat, 74 (B3)
☎ 622 77 82
**Rijksmuseum. Trams 6, 7, 10
Open every day 10am-6pm
and by appt.**

Continuing the tradition of Dutch master glassworkers, this antique shop houses an extraordinary collection of 16th and 17th-century European glass.

The selection of engraved glasses is particularly fine. They were originally given as gifts to mark a special occasion, such as a christening, wedding or birthday. There are many beautiful pieces of Italian or Flemish origin, as well as a large collection of period Dutch faience.

To get an idea of antiques prices, why not have a look round Sotheby's? This famous British firm of auctioneers also has a branch in Amsterdam. Here you'll find sales catalogues showing the prices various items reached at auction. If you'd like to buy something at one of these sales, all items are put on display beforehand.
Sotheby's, Rokin, 102 (B3)
☎ 550 22 00
Open Mon.-Fri. 9am-5pm.

OLD BOOKS AND BRIC-A-BRAC

Bric-a-brac is a tradition in Holland and is sold in all the city's markets. But you'll find the real bargains in the antique shops, where they may be a bit dearer but there's less doubt about authenticity. There are also a great many secondhand booksellers, heirs to a long-standing tradition of book-collecting. As upholders of tolerance, the Dutch for a long time published books that were banned elsewhere.

Fifties-Sixties

Huidenstraat, 13 (B3)
☎ **623 26 53**
Spui
Trams 1, 2, 5, 11
Open Tue.-Sat.
1-6pm.

You'll find the owner of this shop, who guarantees the authenticity of her stock from the 1930s-60s, surrounded by a charming jumble of lighting equipment and household electrical goods.

A fine selection of kitchen gadgets, crockery and lamps in absolutely unrepeatable designs and not too expensive. Not all of it would look right in any home, but fans of sixties retro will be in seventh heaven. Expect to pay 275Fl for a 1940 Philips lamp, 165Fl for a 1950 toaster.

& Klevering

Bloemgracht, 175-177 (A1)
☎ **422 03 97**
Tue.-Fri. 11am-6pm, Sat. 10.30am-5.30pm.

A warehouse laid out around a superb wrought-iron staircase, selling period materials and antiques, mainly from France and Spain. Give your interior decor a comparatively cheap period makeover with items from among the bathtubs, heaters, display cases, lamps and wardrobes on display. For those nostalgic for the early 19th century,.

Puck

Nieuwe Hoogstraat, 1 (corner of Kloveniersburgwal – C2)
Metro Nieuwmarkt
Open Mon.-Sat. 11am-6pm.

Lovers of retro clothes will find clothes to wear at any time of day or night – lace nightgown (30Fl), lingerie, lacy bodices (20Fl), evening dress with straps and sequins (115Fl) with period costume jewellery to match. Homemade, embroidered linens and period crockery are also on sale in this retro cornucopia.

Tut-Tut

Elandsgracht, 109 (De Looier antiekmarkt – A2)
☎ **627 79 60**
Trams 7, 10
Open Thu.-Sat. 11am-5pm, Thu. until 9pm.

Among the antique-sellers in this little market is a stall specialising in old toys – robots, mechanical toys, and Fleischmann, Dinky and Matchbox trains (sometimes in the original box). Be prepared to haggle!

Conny Mol

Elandsgracht, 65 (A2)
☎ **623 25 36**
Trams 7, 10
Open Wed.-Sat. 11am-6pm.

Conny Mol is interested in furniture, lighting equipment and objects dating from 1850 to 1945. In the large range here, you'll find

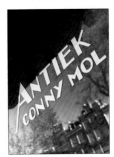

lovely Art Deco pieces, as well as a wide choice of mirrors at around 150Fl. You might even find that sofa in leopard-skin velvet that you've always wanted to add the finishing touch to your living-room.

Meulendijks & Schuil

**Nieuwe Spiegelstraat 45a
(not on map)
☎ 620 03 00
Mon.-Sat. 9am-9pm.**

An address to remember for all sailing fanatics and people interested in the beginnings of the science of navigation, with old compasses, 18th-century sextants and chronometers. Loads of decorative and gift ideas, often less expensive than you'd expect.

Keystone Novelty Store

**Huidenstraat, 28 (B3)
☎ 625 26 60
Spui. Trams 1, 2, 5, 11
Open Tue.-Sat. 10.30am-6pm.**

Lovers of old toys will be amazed by the range in this shop, which also sells crockery and household

electrical appliances from the 1950s. Dinky Toys at 10Fl each, a Fleischmann locomotive for 385Fl and mechanical dolls for 75Fl each. Great prices for nostalgic grown-ups and plenty of choice for toy collectors.

Silverplate

**Nes, 89 (B2). ☎ 624 83 39
Mon. noon-6pm, Tue.-Wed. 11am-6pm, Sat. 11am-5pm.**

A stone's throw from Rokin, Kyra ten Kate has opened a shop where you can buy 19th-century silverware and silver plate pieces for a really elegant dinner table. A wide choice of both cutlery and dinner service items.

Singel 91

**Singel, 91 (5 mins from central station – B2)
☎ 420 05 03
Open Thu.-Fri. noon-6pm,**

Sat. 10am-6pm, Sun. noon-5pm.

Here you'll find beautiful, unusual pieces of furniture (large wardrobe at 1,900Fl) imported from India. Besides the pine and teak tables there's a great number of mirrors, copies of 19th-century pieces, and some items for boats and ships. No pieces of real 'bourgeois' furniture, but a fine selection of often highly decorative desks, armchairs and writing desks.

DE ROMMELMARKT (BRIC-A-BRAC MARKET)

**Looiersgracht, 38 (A3)
Trams 7, 10
Open Sat.-Thu. 11am-5pm.**

A few stalls indicate the entrance to this covered market on two floors, with two hundred permanent or occasional stands dealing in bric-a-brac. If you want to find that special bargain, your best chance is at the weekend.

TOBACCO AND SPIRITS

The Dutch are known for their love of good tobacco and their production (and consumption) of quality alcoholic drinks, so it's hardly surprising that Amsterdam has a great number of shops devoted to these forbidden fruits. You'll also find shops selling spices, full of scents reminiscent of hot and exotic Indonesia, reminders of Amsterdam's past, at the centre of a colonial empire.

P.G.C. Hajenius
Rokin, 92-96 (B2)
☎ **623 74 94**
Between Dam and Muntplein
Mon. noon-6pm, Tue.-Sat. 9.30-6pm, Thu. until 9pm, Sun. noon-5pm

Even non-smokers should visit this smoker's paradise, where the superb Art Deco interior has remained unchanged since 1914. As soon as you step through the door, your nostrils are assailed by the mingled scents of tobacco. With its period wood-panelling and shelves filled with cigars, pipes and tobacco jars, Hajenius is a chic and classy shop, with a touch of old-fashioned stuffiness that's rather amusing, and has been renowned for 170 years for the subtle mix of flavours in its cigars, from cigarillos to coronas.

You can also buy every kind of luxury accessory for smokers here – lighters, boxes, humidifiers, cigar cases and a colossal choice of earthenware, wooden and meerschaum pipes.

Herboristerie Jacob Hooy & Co
Kloveniersburgwal, 10-12
☎ **624 30 41**
Metro Nieuwmarkt (C2)
Open Mon. noon-6pm, Tue.-Fri. 8am-6pm, Sat. 8am-5pm.

It's now the fifth generation of Oldenbooms who stand behind the antique counter that has been in their family for a hundred and fifty years. Their shop specialises in medicinal herbs and spices (six hundred varieties), natural cosmetic products and sweets, including their famous licorice drops. Even if you decide not to buy anything, the shop is worth visiting just to see its shelves full of jars.

Homeopatheek De Munt
Vijzelstraat, 1 (B3)
☎ **624 45 33**
Muntplein
Open Mon.-Sat. 9.30am-6pm.

This little shop is filled with the smell of spices and the perfume of delicately-composed pot-pourris of dried flowers, which you can use to give your home a subtle background scent. These skilful combinations of colour and perfume, at once discreet and very decorative, will give your interior a touch of class. Also in this shop you'll find a very wide range of medicinal plants and licorice sweets.

Van Coeverden
Leidsestraat, 58 (B3)
☎ **624 51 50**
Trams 1, 2, 5, 11
Open Mon.-Sat. 10am-6pm.

A real old-fashioned tobacco shop, with a tiled floor and dark, wooden shelves filled with pipes, cigar boxes, packets of rolling tobacco and even cigarettes. The walls themselves seem to be impregnated with the smell of tobacco. Nothing here seems to have changed much for decades and, even if you're not crazy about cigarettes, it's worth stepping inside just to experience the atmosphere of one of these shops that are so typical of Amsterdam.

De Bierkoning

Paleisstraat, 125 (B2)
☎ 625 23 36
Dam
Open Mon. 1-6.30pm,
Tue.-Fri. 11am-6.30pm,
Thu. until 9pm,
Sat. 11am-6pm.

However short your stay in Amsterdam, don't let it pass by without visiting a brasserie or other establishment for beer-drinking. This liquid has been flowing in Amsterdam's cafés since the 16th century. In De Bierkoning you'll find a selection of 850 different kinds of beer, to drink on the premises or take away. And for purists, there's an appropriate glass to go with every type.

Oud Amsterdam

Nieuwendijk, 75
☎ 624 45 81
Dam
Open Mon.-Sat. 10am-6pm.

In this very busy shopping street, Oud Amsterdam ('Old Amsterdam') is an old-fashioned shop with beams decorated with

little bottles of spirits. Behind the counter , with its patina of age, you can see the fifty or so Dutch liqueurs, and particularly the seventeen types of *jenever* distilled here and aged for 1 to 17 years. Tasting essential.

Henri Bloem's

Gravenstraat, 8 (B2)
☎ 623 08 86
Dam
Open Mon. noon-6pm, Tue.-Fri. 10am-6pm, Thu. until 9pm, Sat. 10am-5.30pm.

This is more than just a shop selling spirits. Here you'll find someone who can really tell you all about the various *jenevers* and the subtle differences between *bessenjenever*, *oude jenever* and *korenwijn*. After that, you'll be able to buy with the confidence of a true connoisseur.

JENEVER OR BRANDY?

Jenever is flavoured with herbs and can be drunk young or old. It can also be distilled with lemon or redcurrants. Many people also enjoy the fruit brandies, such as *'Rose sans épines'* ('Rose without thorns'), made by monks, or *Oranje Bitter*, a syrupy orange liqueur which is drunk on 30 April, when the birthday of Queen Beatrix is celebrated.

COFFEE, TEA, CHOCOLATE AND SPICES

Would you like an *Amsterdammertje* or a *speculaasje* with your coffee? If you don't want to look like an ignoramus when faced with this kind of question, be sure to make an early visit to one of Amsterdam's excellent confectioners to sample the subtle flavours of bitter chocolate and ginger biscuits. Then savour the aroma of freshly-ground coffee emanating from one of the old cafés, most of which were founded at the time of the East India Company's first expeditions to the spice islands of the Far East. And if you'd like to try your hand at Indonesian cooking, south Amsterdam is the place to go for the greatest range of exotic ingredients.

Geels & Co

(see p. 47).
Warmoesstraat, 67 (C2)
☎ **624 06 83**
Dam
Open Mon.-Sat 9.30am-5pm.

Founded 140 years ago, this family business in the heart of the red light district grinds 20 different types of coffee on the premises. A delicious smell and a charming shop, where the boxes and jars look like something out of a 1930s film set. Worth a detour.

Simon Lévelt

Prinsengracht, 180 (A1)
☎ **624 08 23**
Westerkerk
Open Mon. noon-6pm,
Tue.-Fri. 9am-6pm,
Sat. 9am-5pm.

Since 1839 this lovely shop decorated with wrought iron and

situated opposite the Westerkerk has been selling 25 sorts of coffee, ground on the premises, and 100 special blends of tea. Don't miss.

Wijs & Zonen

Warmoesstraat, 102 (C2)
☎ **624 04 36**
Dam
Open Mon.-Fri. 9am-
5.30pm, Sat. 10am-5.30pm.

A pretty little shop with a lovely smell of coffee, which is kept in enamelled jars. Generations have watched the repetition of the same ritual, when a taster comes to verify the standard of the subtle blends of forty different kinds of tea.

Puccini Bomboni

Singel, 184 (corner of Oud Leliestraat – B1)
☎ **427 83 41**
Dam
Open Tue.-Sat. 10am-6pm,
Sun. 1-6pm.

In the centre of this beautiful shop, where the light falls through stained-glass windows, exquisite chocolates are piled in delicately-balanced pyramids on the counter. Ans van Soelen makes them using butter and cocoa, to old-fashioned

recipes, without preservatives. Truly delicious. Not for weight watchers!

Toko Ramee

Ferdinand Bolstraat, 74 (not on map)
☎ 662 20 25
Trams 16, 24, 25
Open Tue.-Fri. 9am-6pm, Sat. 9am-5pm.

Krupuk, ayam, sambal, gado gado, bami, nasi – you could play a guessing game, trying to match these Indonesian names to products. On the other hand, if you want to buy with confidence, you'd be better off asking the advice of the charming Moluccan lady who sells the spices and can also explain to you how to use them when you're cooking chicken or pork. So why not bring a hint of adventure to your cooking? You can, of course, also use these ingredients very successfully to spice up western-style food.

Arnold Cornelis

Elandsgracht, 78 (A2)
☎ 625 85 85
Jordaan. Trams 7, 10.
Also Van Baerlestraat, 93
☎ 618 36 88
Museums. Trams 3, 5, 12
Open Mon.-Fri. 9am-6pm, Sat. 9am-5pm.

In this renowned patisserie you'll find not just delicious fruit tarts

(Limburgse vlaai), but also confectionery, butter biscuits, *speculaas* – delicious with coffee – marzipan and chocolate, all of them homemade. The greedy Amsterdamer's favourite shop.

Diva Bonbon!

Prins Hendrikkade, 60 (C1)
☎ 422 30 00
Mon.-Sat. 9am-9pm.

Service with a smile in this little royal-blue and red shop, all spick and span and situated just a stone's throw from Centraal Station. Here you can sample chocolates of all shapes, colours and, above all, flavours. Make sure you try the Brussels sprouts – not a green vegetable, but a subtle combination of white chocolate and almonds.

Chocolaterie Internationaal

Nieuwe Spiegelstraat, 1 (by Herengracht – B3)
Open Mon. noon-5.30pm, Tue.-Sat. 9.30am-5.30pm, Sun. 10.30am-5.30pm.

Among all the delicious things on offer, make sure you try the dark or milk chocolate drops which have been made by Droste for several generations. The *Amsterdammertjes* chocolates, shaped like Amsterdam bollards

THE TRIALS AND TRIBULATIONS OF COFFEE

Did you know that the name coffee comes from *Kaffa*, a region in Ethiopia where the coffee tree comes from? When Arab merchants introduced the drink to Yemen, it became known as *Arabica* or *Moka*, the name of the port from which most of it was exported. In 1714 Pancras, Mayor of Amsterdam, gave King Louis XIV of France a few coffee plants, which the Dutch had acclimatised in their Indonesian colony of Batavia. The French then took them to Guyana and Brazil.

(yes, bollards!) are also famous and prettily presented in boxes. And don't miss out on the *Haagse hopjes* (coffee caramels) and *Zeeuwse babbelaars* (salted butter caramels), a wonderful speciality from Zeeland and a great gift idea for the sweet-toothed.

SECONDHAND GOODS

The Dutch love a bargain. For secondhand clothes, go to the markets on Waterlooplein and Noordermarkt, where the great revival of 1970s clothes is in full swing. If you prefer more of a classic look, it's better to go to the specialist shops in Jordaan. Many shops in Kalverstraat and Nieuwendijk have sales on all year round. And, like everywhere else, the smartest time to buy is when you see posters in the windows proclaiming *'Uitverkoop'* or *'Opruiming'*. Sales are held twice a year, starting in the last weeks of December and June and continuing for about a month.

Jo-Jo Outfitters and Jo-Jo Shop

Huidenstraat, 23 (B3)
☎ 623 34 76
Spui. Trams 1, 2, 5.
Runstraat, 9 (A3)
☎ 624 40 02
Open Mon. noon-6pm,
Tue.-Fri. 11am-6pm,
Sat. 11am-5.30pm.

For men (Huidenstraat) or women

(Runstraat), unlabelled British and American brands. Quality and durability are the watchwords, with Burberry raincoats at 95Fl and shirts from 15 to 25Fl. Nothing very imaginative, but they're all good quality items you can keep on wearing.

De Rits

Prinsengracht, 484 (A3)
☎ 627 25 73
Leidsestraat
Trams 1, 2, 5, 11
Open Mon.-Sat. noon-8pm.

Secondhand clothing for men only, with leather jackets at 150Fl and shirts at 10Fl. The sportswear and classic clothing on sale is cheap, but smells slightly of cooking, since the owner makes his dinner here every day at 6pm precisely.

Callas 43

Haarlemmerdijk, 43 (not on map)
☎427 37 90
Spui. Trams 1, 2, 5
Open Mon.-Sat. noon-6pm.

Luxury secondhand gear, with clothing, jewellery and accessories by Karl Lagerfeld, YSL, Dior, Edgar Vos and other prestige brands for a third of the price. A very popular shop where you can find real bargains. Some think this alone justifies their trip. An address to keep under your hat.

Pakhuis Amerika

Prinsengracht, 541 (A1)
☎ 639 25 83
Open Thu.-Sat. 11am-6pm.

Exclusively American secondhand items. Look no further if you want to buy a good old sofa, a chrome letterbox, real cowboy boots, an authentic G.I. uniform, a formica table or even a rocking chair.

This is a real pilgrimage to the heart of America, from the backest of backwoods to the heights and depths of New York. Visit essential.

John Fiets Inn

Spinozastraat, 2 (not on map)
☎ 428 43 85
Metro Westerplein
Mon.-Sat. 7.30am-7pm.

Sugar pink, leopard skin, with a child seat or a basket to carry your dog, however you like your bicycle, this is the place for a bargain. Dutch *Gazelle* and *Batavus* bikes are on sale for 275Fl secondhand (in other words half the price of a new one) and, unlike the market, you can be sure you're not buying someone else's stolen vehicle here. If you really want to go Dutch, of

course, you need one with a backpedal brake.

Laura Dols en de Verkleed Komeet

Wolvenstraat, 7 (B2), ☎ 624 90 66
Every day 11am-6pm, Thu. until 9pm.

Here fans of 1940s and 50s nostalgia will find everything they could wish for to dress themselves from head to toe. From beautiful satin slips to a hat with a veil and matching gloves and handbag, there's an amazingly wide choice at amazingly low prices (crocodile-skin bag at 30Fl, hat 25Fl). Loads of gift ideas, such as toilet requisites in a kid case, wonderful costume jewellery and horn-rimmed sunglasses.

Second Best

Wolvenstraat, 18 (B2)
☎ 422 02 74
Mon. 1-6pm, Tue.-Fri. 11am-6pm, Sat. 11am-5pm.

Clothes that have hardly been worn, jettisoned by fashion photographers, designers and the idle rich when they're updating their wardrobes. In other words, this is absolutely the place to find the leather coat you've always dreamed of, a practically new pair of Prada shoes or some really wild lingerie. Allow 300-350Fl for an ensemble with a designer label, 160Fl for a leather jacket and 60Fl for a pair of trousers.

Zipper

Huidenstraat, 7 (B3)
☎ 623 73 02
Spui. Trams 1, 2, 5
Open Tue.-Fri. 11am-6pm, Sat. 11am-5pm.

A great selection of clothing for 20-30 year-olds at amazing prices, with slightly worn jeans, checked flanelette shirts, leather bomber jackets, little floral dresses and flared trousers. At Zipper you can construct a total seventies look for next to nothing. Of course, if you're over forty, you'd be better off going elsewhere.

Nightlife Practicalities

Whether you're a music or theatre fan or just a night-owl, Amsterdam will fulfil all your expectations. Nightlife is concentrated in three districts, winter and summer.

Full of restaurants, theatres, bars and jazz clubs, Leidseplein is the haunt of young, fairly well-behaved people. In the red light district around the station, with its neon signs, women on display in shop windows, shady bars and countless sex shops, life goes on all night long, attracting a crowd of voyeuristic tourists, dealers and customers. But the real heartbeat of the Amsterdam night can be heard around Rembrandtplein. This is where you'll find the coolest bars, the weirdest clubs and the wildest people, where gays rub shoulders with students, foreigners and Amsterdam's upper crust, who can be observed out slumming it with the rest. Here too, if you want to, you can dance all night long to the deafening sound of techno and house.

As soon as the weather improves, the streets are filled with music and musical events, most of which you can enjoy for nothing. There are open air rock, pop and jazz concerts and brass bands, particularly in Vondelpark and Amsterdamse Bos. Classical music also takes to the streets, settling on the barges moored along the canalsides or invading Jordaan.

CAFÉS

Around 8pm the beer and spirits start to flow. Barriers between different sections of society come down in the cafés, where Amsterdammers prefer to spend their evenings out, and where they can sit every night till 1am and till 2 or 3am on Friday and Saturday nights. From the unpretentious local cafés, where the customers sometimes break into song, to the 'brown cafés', where they drink strong beers with *jenever* chasers, to the cool cafés, where the young people gather before going off to dance all night, to the coffee-shops for whacky weed-lovers, to gay bars where leather gear is the rule, there's an enormous choice and you can easily move from one ambiance to another. They're all next to each other and you'll get a warm welcome in all of them.

NIGHTLIFE AMSTERDAM-STYLE

Don't bother with a classy wardrobe if you're going out in Amsterdam. The ambiance is relaxed

everywhere you go, and that goes for even the smartest, most prestigious places, such as the Muziektheather or Concertgebouw. Older people might want to wear an evening dress or a suit, but it's certainly not obligatory and you'll be allowed in without. You don't even have to wear a tie in the casino, though they do draw the line at shorts and trainers. And at the hippest clubs, the more original, amusing and cool you look, the more likely it is the bouncer will let you in.

DISCOS AND JAZZ CLUBS

The clubs open their doors at 11pm, but don't expect to find many people there that early. Before going to their favourite clubs, Amsterdammers do a tour of the cafés, setting off to dance around 1am and generally staying on till closing-time (4am on week nights and 5am on Friday and Saturday nights). It will cost you between 5 and 20Fl to get in, depending on what day it is, and no-one gets any special treatment. The door price sometimes includes the cost of a membership card, which enables you to go again another night. Bands start playing in the jazz clubs and music cafés around 9pm. You can get in for nothing as long as you buy drinks.

All year round there are concerts of every kind, from rock, pop and world music to classical and chamber music, as well as theatre, dance, opera and cabaret in a huge variety of places from the plain to the magnificent.

To find the evening to suit you among the hundreds of events on offer every week, look at the posters and read the montly magazine *Uitkrant*, which is published by the AUB and is available in bookshops, cafés and tourist information offices. It's written in Dutch, but provides a complete calendar of cultural events. There's a free supplement called *Pop & jazz Uitlijst*, which comes out twice a week and gives you all the information about rock, blues and jazz concerts and what's on in the clubs. There's also an English-language *What's on*, published monthly by the VVV and providing day-by-day information on the main events on offer, including music, theatre and ballet. This is distributed free in all good hotels.

TICKETS

Although the most prestigious early music concerts, operas and ballets are usually sold out weeks in advance, it's often possible to get tickets the day before, or on the night itself, though you shouldn't expect to get a very good seat.

Unless it's a last-minute decision, don't bother to go to the concert hall or theatre to book your seats. The central booking office of the AUB (Amsterdams Uit Buro) Leidseplein, 26, near the Stadsschouwburg, is open daily (including Sundays) 10am-6pm and until 9pm Thursdays. The 3Fl commission is also charged by the booking offices in the venues themselves and all credit cards are accepted. Remember that pre-booking for the same evening closes at 4pm. After that you have to go to the venue itself, where tickets are sold until an hour before the event starts. Seats that have been booked and paid for will be resold if not collected an hour before the curtain rises.

BOOKING TICKETS BY PHONE

If you have a credit card, you can also make your booking from your hotel by calling the Uitlijn, which is open daily. 9am–9pm
☎ 0900 0191 (75ct per min). (6Fl commision).

The VVV offices also handle bookings, but you have to go there in person. (Leidseplein, 106 or Stationplein, 10).

CONCERTS, THEATRE, CABARET, OPERA AND DANCE

Concertgebouw

Concertgebouwplein, 2-6
☎ 573 05 73
Trams 2, 3, 5, 12
Booking 10am-7pm
Tickets 20/25Fl
**Concerts begin at 8.15pm
or 8.30pm**
**For concerts that are sold
out in advance, contact INFO-
LINE ☎ 675 44 11, which
provides information about
the number of seats that will
be available on the day.**

This hall, which is renowned
for the quality of its acoustics,
is the home of the Royal
Orchestra of the Netherlands,
conducted by Riccardo Chailly.
This temple to classical music
stages concerts by the greatest
early music ensembles, especially
Baroque music.

Beurs van Berlage

Damrak, 277 (C2)
☎ 627 04 66 (Dam)
Booking Mon.-Sat. 12.30-6pm
Concerts begin at 8.30pm
Tickets 17.50Fl.

This is home to the
Philharmonic orchestra of the
Netherlands, as well as the
National Orchestra of Chamber
Music. Concerts by other classical
music ensembles are also staged
here in the prestigious setting of
a monument symbolic of Dutch
Art Nouveau.

Muziektheater

Amstel, 3 (C3)
☎ 625 54 55
Metro Waterlooplein
**Booking Mon.-Sat. 10am-
7pm**
Tickets 25-110 Fl
**Concerts begin at 7.30pm or
8.15pm.**

The new Stopera complex, which
opened in 1988, seats up to 1,600
spectators. The national ballet
and the Netherlands Opera are
based here and stage fairly
eclectic programmes ranging
from classical works to
new productions.

Stadschouwburg

Leidseplein, 26 (A3)
☎ 523 77 00
Trams 1, 2, 5, 7, 10
**Booking Mon.-Sat. 10am-
6.30pm**
**Curtain rises at 8.15pm.
tickets 20-40Fl.**

The Stadschouwburg stages
music, as well as theatre and
contemporary dance, performed
by companies from the
Netherlands and other countries.

Koninklijk Theater Carré

Amstel, 115-125 (C3)
☎ 622 52 25.

Since 1887 this former circus hall has provided a venue for grand spectaculars of all kinds, including circuses and a variety of musical shows.

Nieuwe de la Mar Theater

Marnistraat, 404 (not on map)
☎ 530 53 02. Trams 7, 10.

This theatre specialises in cabaret and popular music and dance from around the world.

De IJsbreker

Weesperzijde, 23 (not on map)
☎ 668 18 05
Metro Weesperplein
Concerts begin at 8.30pm and 4.30pm on Sun.

This hall by the Amstel is the home of contemporary music (John Cage, Mauricio Kagel, Salvatore Sciarrino and Georg Katzer), with concerts of accordeon music, electronic music and various experimental groups.

Het Soeterijn

Linnaeusstraat, 2 (not on map)
☎ 568 85 00. Trams 9, 14.

This little theatre attached to the Tropenmuseum prides itself on providing a stage for non-western culture. Its programme includes southern Moroccan music, classical Arab and Indian music and Asian theatre and dance.

Felix Meritis Theatre

Keizersgracht, 324 (B1)
☎ 623 13 11. Trams 1, 2,5
Curtain rises at 8.30pm.

English-language avant-garde plays are performed in the prestigious setting of this theatre, which first opened in 1787. Modern dance productions are also staged here.

Nieuwe Kerk

Dam (B2), ☎ 638 69 09
Entry charge 12.5Fl.

Every Sunday evening from July to the end of September there's a concert of organ music in the grand setting of the New Church. The programme includes works by Bach, Mendelssohn, Purcell and Buxtehude

Classical music concerts are also staged in Vondelpark, the English and Walloon churches of the Béguinage convent, the van Loon museum, the Bethany cloister, St. Nicolas's church, the Oude kerk and the large hall in the Tropenmuseum.

CASINO

Holland Casino Amsterdam

Max Euweplein, 62 (not on map), ☎ 620 10 06
Open daily 1.30pm-2am.
Entrance fee 6Fl.

If you're tempted by roulette, Black Jack or poker, why not go to the new casino near Leidseplein? The building is nothing special but the fever gripping the gamblers is the same as in older casinos. The café-restaurant on the lower floor has a lovely waterside terrace and stages cabaret shows from Wednesday to Sunday, starting at 6.30pm. You can also waltz to the sound of the orchestra.

A PICTURESQUE EVENING WALK IN THE AMSTELVELD

This walk around the locality of bustling Rembrandtplein, where the many cafés stay open and busy late into the night, takes you along the canals and by the banks of the River Amstel, from which the city takes its name. What better way to explore Amsterdam after dark, from the friendly buzz of the cafés to the quiet poetry of the silent canals?

STARTING FROM REMBRANDTPLEIN

This old square used to be home to the butter market and didn't receive the name it has today until the late 19th century, when a bronze statue of the famous 17th-century artist was put up in the centre. In summer the café terraces are full and the competing sounds of music echo all round the square. Leave all this bustle behind and walk down Amstelsraat to the Blue Bridge (*Blauwbrug*).

THE BANKS OF THE AMSTEL

Instead of a canal, you come to the banks of a river, which has been lined with dykes because it flows below sea level here. The Blue Bridge (see p. 49), takes its name from the wooden bridge, painted blue, that used to cross the Amstel at this point. The bridge you see today dates from the end of the 19th century. Its finely-wrought candelabra stand on sculpted bases, representing ships' prows.

Keep walking along the river bank in a southerly direction. Three hundred metres/yds further down you come to the Skinny Bridge (*Magere Brug*), one of the last bascule bridges in the city and the one most loved by Amsterdammers. It was enlarged slightly when it was restored in 1969, but its shape remains largely unchanged. You can spot it at night by the lights along its arches and balancing arms.

KOKADORUS AND AMSTELKERK

Cross Utrechtsestraat and keep walking along Prinsengracht until you come to the little square with the statue of Kokadorus, a famously silver-tongued stallholder who sold his wares in the little market held here until the beginning of the 20th century. Next to you you can see the Amstelkerk church, the oldest wooden church in Amsterdam. When it was built, it was intended to be temporary, but it was never replaced by a permanent structure because the clergy were unable to raise enough money to pay for it.

Go down Kerkstraat, which will take you back to Utrechtstraat. At the end of the street you will see the bright lights of Rembrandtplein once more.

PRINSENGRACHT

Keep walking along the river Amstel until you come to Prinsengracht – the Canal of Princes – and turn right to walk along it. After the river bank, which is always quite busy and lively, you suddenly plunge into a much calmer, quieter world, where it seems that everyone and everything is fast asleep.

people turn their lights on after dark, you can see how very large the windows are. Often, at the front of the rooms, there's more glass than brick. This is to let in as much daylight as possible. In the same way, because Amsterdam isn't a very sunny city, the windows are set flush with the wall, whereas in hotter places they tend to be more deeply recessed.

The Dutch are less concerned with privacy than many other nations and many of their windows have neither shutters nor curtains. Even if you aren't usually given to voyeurism, when the lights come on take the opportunity to have a look at the interiors, which are often very tastefully decorated. An evening walk also enables you to notice some of the characteristic features of the architecture of houses in Amsterdam. For example, when

CAFÉS

As well as the cafés mentioned on p. 28-29, which are open until 1-2am, here are some ideas for places which often have live music on Friday and Saturday nights and where snacks and light meals are served until midnight or 1am.

De Engelbewaarder

Kloveniersburgwal, 59 (C2)
☎ 625 37 72.

A very relaxed atmosphere in this friendly café which is the haunt of many newspaper people. Sunday is jazz day, when jazz-lovers come to enjoy the afternoon jam-sessions.

De Twee Zwaantjes

Prinsengracht, 114 (A1)
☎ 625 27 29.

A typical Jordaan 'brown café' and former meeting-place for local brewers and workmen. Live music at weekends, or when the customers do the singing. A mixed crowd and very 'Jordaan' atmosphere – in other words working-class and fun.

Mulligan's

Amstel, 100 (C3)
☎ 622 13 30. Trams 4, 9, 14.

An atmosphere of heat and alcohol fumes in this Irish pub with live folk groups playing Celtic music at the weekends. Popular with the Irish, of course.

Dulac

Haarlemmerstraat, 118 (B1)
☎ 624 42 65. Bus 18, 22.

A large, smarter café near the central station, decorated in a skilful blend of Art Deco and neo-Gothic, with live jazz groups on a Saturday night and Sunday afternoon.

Café Cox

Marnixstraat, 429 (A2)
☎ 620 72 22.

Favourite haunt of actors and directors from the Stadsschouwburg next door. The kitchen is open until half-past midnight.

De Balie

Kleine Gartmanplantsoen, 10 (not on map), ☎ 553 51 30.

This large café near Leidseplein, is the locals' favourite stop after the cinema or theatre or before the clubs. Snacks and light meals until 1am.

Van Puffelen

Prinsengracht, 377 (A2)
☎ 624 62 70.

Cosy atmosphere, candlelight and, if you're peckish, light meals of Italian and French dishes.

POP, ROCK, BLUES & JAZZ CLUBS

Alto

**Korte Leidsedwarsstraat, 115
(Leidseplein – not on map)
☎ 626 32 49. Every night
9pm-3am, 4am weekends.**

Different types of band play live in this jazz club. Very lively jam session on Wednesdays with Hans Dulfer, one of the pillars of the Amsterdam jazz scene. Hein van der Haag plays piano on Mondays.

Akhnaton

**Nieuwezijds Kolk, 25
(Beurs – B1) ☎ 624 33 96
Open Fri and Sat from 11pm,
Sun from 3pm.**

Fans of salsa, lambada and other Latino-African rhythms meet here every Friday. Live bands also play here.

Bamboo Bar

**Lange Leidsedwarsstraat, 66
(not on map),
☎ 624 39 93.**

Jazz and blues bands play live every night after 10pm in pseudo tropical surroundings.

Bimhuis

**Oude Schans, 73-77
☎ 623 13 61
Metro Nieuwmarkt.**

Jazz temple where the greatest international jazz musicians come to play. Free jam sessions on Mondays, Tuesdays and Fridays. Tickets 25Fl for live bands Thursday to Saturday.

Bourbon Street

**Leidsekruisstraat, 6
(Leidseplein – A3)
☎ 623 34 40
Every night 10pm-4am,
5am at weekends.**

A varied, good quality programme of pop, rock, jazz and blues artists. Jeff Healey and Sting have played here.

Cruise Inn

**Zeeburgerdijk, 271-273
(not on map)
☎ 692 71 88.**

Fans of good ol' fifties jive and rock 'n roll gather here every Saturday night for some acrobatic dancing.

Casablanca

**Zeedijk, 26 (C1)
☎ 625 56 85.**

A jazz café with live bands Mondays to Wednesdays after 9pm. From Thursday to Saturday the place is given over to the joys of karaoke.

Paradiso

**Weteringschans,
6-8 (Leidseplein –
A3), ☎ 626 45 21
Membership card required
(5Fl), tickets 7.50- 35Fl
depending on band.
Doors open 10pm.**

When it ceased to be used as a church, this old building became the haunt of hippies, who came to sit in clouds of incense and marijuana smoke listening to Indian music. Now it has become a venue for all kinds of music, from modern classical works to Mexican Mariachis, electronic, funk, jazz and salsa sounds. VIP nights on Fridays and 'Paradisco' on Saturdays for those who still want to come here to dance.

De Westergasfabriek

**Haarlemmerweg, 8-10 (not
on map), ☎ 581 04 25
Tram 10.**

This former gasworks is now the venue for all kinds of cultural

events themed around the future, with exhibitions, fashion shows, pop, rock and jazz bands and a discotheque in the West Pacific restaurant.

De Melkweg

Lijnbaansgracht, 234 (Leidseplein)
☎ 624 17 77
Membership card required (4Fl), tickets 7.50-25Fl depending on the show
Doors open 10pm.

In a sign of the times, this former dairy near Leidseplein, which was once the capital of seventies rock music and the hippies' gathering-place, has had a total makeover. Today it's a venue for film shows, pop and world music gigs, avant-garde theatre productions and even a restaurant. For the nostalgic, there's still a disco at weekends, with differents DJs hosting theme nights.

Blitz

Reguliersdwarsstraat, 45 (C3)
☎ 622 66 82.

A large aluminium bar with a dance-floor upstairs. A meeting-place for yuppies from Amsterdam and elsewhere, who come to drink explosive cocktails set alight in the glass. Good DJs on Thursday, Friday and Saturday nights.

NIGHTCLUBS

iT

Amstelstraat, 24 (Rembrandtplein).

The most outrageous club in Amsterdam where, once inside, you have to abandon all your inhibitions. House music and a very hot ambiance. A great place to pose if that's what takes your fancy. But don't worry, you can just come to dance. Saturday is gay night.

Arena

's-Gravesandestraat, 51 (2km from town, well-connected by public transport)
☎ 694 74 44
Open Thu. 11pm-4am, Fri.-Sat. 11pm-5am

Housed in a former convent, this multi-purpose cultural centre hosts club nights on Fridays and dance events at the weekend, often with well-known guest DJs and performers. Admission 10-15Fl.

Sandy's

Reguliersdwarsstraat, 16 (C3)
☎ 421 26 65.

Famous DJs mix the latest sounds while beautiful girls pour the drinks and the dance floor heaves with clubbers wearing the latest fashions. You'll need to wear your trendy gear rather than casual sportswear.

Odeon

Singel, 460 (behind flower market – B3).

The young, smart and comparatively staid come to this very cosy former residential home, with its painted ceilings and large mirrors, for a choice of jazz in the cellar, retro music

on the first floor and DJs in the hall of mirrors.

Escape-Chemistry

Rembrandtplein, 11 (C3).

The crowd consists mainly of teenagers at this mega disco. The ambiance depends on what the DJ plays, but it's mostly somewhere between rap and the Smurfs, or commercial house music. Not for the over-30s!

Mazzo

Rozengracht, 114 (A2)
Trams 13, 14, 17.

Very relaxed ambiance with a young crowd who like urban dance music – rap, hip-hop, acid, and techno. London bands play live on Friday nights.

Havana

Reguliersdwarsstraat, 17-19 (behind the flower market – B3).

A bar and club where gays go to drink, talk, meet people and dance, after dinner until 1am, or 2am at weekends.

Soul Kitchen

Amstelstraat, 32 (Rembrandtplein – C3).

For fans of 60s and 70s music, soul, funk and jazz in lovely surroundings. Membership card required.

More handy words and phrases

Almost everybody speaks English in Holland. However, it's always nice to make an effort to speak the language, but don't be put off when the reply is in English; Amsterdam people are used to speaking with foreigners.

In Dutch, like in other European languages, there is a formal and an informal way to address people; 'u' is formal (strangers, superiors) and 'je' (younger people, friends) informal.

AT THE HOTEL
double bed
tweepersoonsbed
room with two beds
een kamer met twee bedden
en-suite bathroom
privé badkamer
toilet
toilet *or* wc
with air conditioning
met airconditioning
reservation
reservering
left luggage
bagage depot
case
koffer
bag/handbag/plastic bag
tas/handtas/plastic zak
ground floor
begane grond (*'B' button in lift*)
dining room
eetkamer

MONEY AND BANKING
price
prijs
That's too expensive
Het is te duur
traveller's cheques
travellers' cheques
cash dispensing machine
geldautomaat
I'd like to change some money
Ik wil graag geld wisselen
notes
papiergeld
coins
munten

IN THE RESTAURANT
DRINKS
wine list
wijnkaart
a cup of
een kop
a glass of
een glas
draught beer
bier van de tap
mineral water
Spa rood *(sparkling)*;
Spa blauw *(still) (brand name)*
fruit juice
vruchtensap
milky coffee (café latte)
koffie verkeerd
decaffeinated coffee
cafeïnevrije koffie
hot chocolate
warme chocolademelk
hot aniseed milk
warme anijsmelk
tea *(served weak and black)*
thee *(pronounced: tay)*
herbal tea
kruidenthee
strong tea with milk/lemon
sterke thee met melk/citroen

GENERAL
rice
rijst
egg
ei *(plural:* eieren)
sugar
suiker
salt/pepper
zout/peper

mustard
mosterd
oil
olie

MEAT
meat
vlees
roast
gebraad
baked
gebakken in de oven
grilled
gegrild
poached
gepocheerd
steamed
gestoomd
fried
gebakken
deep fried
gefrituurd
game
wild
steak
biefstuk
chop
koteletje
veal
kalfsvlees
ham
ham
bacon
spek or bacon
roast beef *(on bread)*
rosbief

FISH AND SEAFOOD
shellfish
schaaldieren *or* schelpdieren

mussels
mosselen
cod
kabeljauw
salmon
zalm
trout
forel
sole
tong
plaice
schol
herring
haring
monkfish
zeeduivel
swordfish
zwaardvis
tuna
tonijn
shrimps/prawns
garnalen
lobster
kreeft
smoked eel
gerookte paling

VEGETABLES
potato
aardappel
tomato
tomaat
spinach
spinazie
curly kale
boerenkool
thick carrot
winterpeen
thin baby carrot
worteltje
broad beans
tuinbonen
endive
andijvie
cauliflower
bloemkool
sauerkraut
zuurkool
red cabbage
rode kool
beans
bonen

leek
prei
brussels sprouts
spruitjes
pepper
paprika

FRUIT
fresh fruit
vers fruit
orange
sinaasappel
pear
peer
apple
appel
banana
banaan
plums
pruimen
grapes
druiven
strawberries
aardbeien
raspberries
frambozen
blackberries
bramen

UNDERSTANDING THE MENU
hutspot met klapstuk
mashed potato with carrot, onion and beef
boerenkool met worst
mashed potato with curly kale and smoked sausage
zuurkool met worst
same as above with sauerkraut instead of kale
andijviestamppot
mashed potato with endive and meat
hachee met rode kool en appelmoes
braising steak with onions served with red cabbage and apple sauce
erwtensoep (snert)
thick pea soup with ham
pannenkoek
pancake

rijsttafel
Indonesian 'rice table'
bittergarnituur
platter of various snacks
vlammetjes
little spicy vegetable spring rolls
bitterballen
deep fried ragout in bread-crumbs, served with mustard
kroket
same as bitterballen but bigger, often eaten on bread
haring (Hollandse Nieuwe)
fresh, raw herring
patatje oorlog
chips served with mayonnaise, ketchup and peanut sauce
kaasplankje
cheese platter; the cheese you see everywhere in Holland is 'Gouda' (*not* Edam) which comes in various degrees of ripeness, from young and soft (*jong*) to mature (*belegen*) to very mature and hard (*oud*).

SWEET DISHES
poffertjes
miniature pancakes served with powdery sugar and butter
zoete/zoute drop
sweet/salty liquorice
stroopwafels
syrup waffles
oliebollen
Dutch doughnuts eaten around New Year
appelflappen
apple doughnuts
speculaas
Dutch biscuit baked with spices
ontbijtkoek
breakfast cake with spices

TIME AND PLACE
a week/a month
een week/een maand
minute/hour
minuut/uur
half an hour
een half uur

before/after
voor/na
early/late
vroeg/laat
today/tomorrow
vandaag/morgen
yesterday
gisteren

CLOTHES SHOPPING
belt
riem
boots
laarzen
boutique
winkel
bra
b.h. (bustenhouder)
cotton
katoen
dress
jurk
fashion
mode
hat
hoed
jacket
jas
label
etiket
lace
kantwerk
leather
leer, leder
overcoat
overjas
pullover
trui
raincoat
regenjas
shoes
schoenen
silk
zijde
skirt
rok
socks
sokken
tie
stropdas
underwear
ondergoed

wool
wol

AT CUSTOMS
customs officer
douanier
foreign currencies
vreemde valuta
green card
groene kaart
identity card
identiteitskaart
Anything to declare?
Iets aan te geven?
passport
paspoort
personal possessions
persoonlijke zaken

IN AN EMERGENCY
help
hulp
Help!
Help!
Call a doctor
Roep een dokter
Call the police
Roep de politie
Where is the nearest hospital?
Waar is het dichtstbijzijnde ziekenhuis?
I am ill
Ik ben ziek
aspirin
aspirine

MAKING A PHONE CALL
Where is the nearest telephone?
Waar is de dichtsbijzijnde telefoon?
I would like to make a reverse charge call
Ik wil graag bellen met kosten voor de ontvanger
Can I leave a message
Kan ik een boodschap achterlaten?
I will call back later
Ik bel later terug

IN THE TOWN
left
linksaf
right
rechtsaf
here/there
hier/daar
near/far
dichtbij/ver
straight on
rechtdoor
at the end of
aan het einde van
corner
bocht or hoek
opposite
tegenover
above/below
boven/onder
next to
naast
entrance/exit
ingang/uitgang
prohibited
verboden
no smoking
niet roken
At what time?
Hoe laat?
no entry
geen toegang
I want to go to …
Ik wil naar …
I want to get off at …
Ik wil uitstappen bij …
timetable *(train)*
spoorboekje
on foot
te voet or lopend
taxi rank
taxi standplaats
airport
vliegveld or luchthaven
platform *(train)*
spoor or perron
driver's licence
rijbewijs
I would like to hire a car
Ik wil een auto huren
car hire
autoverhuur

Conversion tables for clothes shopping

Women's sizes

Shirts/dresses

U.K	U.S.A	EUROPE
8	6	36
10	8	38
12	10	40
14	12	42
16	14	44
18	16	46

Sweaters

U.K	U.S.A	EUROPE
8	6	44
10	8	46
12	10	48
14	12	50
16	14	52

Shoes

U.K	U.S.A	EUROPE
3	5	36
4	6	37
5	7	38
6	8	39
7	9	40
8	10	41

Men's sizes

Shirts

U.K	U.S.A	EUROPE
14	14	36
$14^{1}/_{2}$	$14^{1}/_{2}$	37
15	15	38
$15^{1}/_{2}$	$15^{1}/_{2}$	39
16	16	41
$16^{1}/_{2}$	$16^{1}/_{2}$	42
17	17	43
$17^{1}/_{2}$	$17^{1}/_{2}$	44
18	18	46

Suits

U.K	U.S.A	EUROPE
36	36	46
38	38	48
40	40	50
42	42	52
44	44	54
46	46	56

Shoes

U.K	U.S.A	EUROPE
6	8	39
7	9	40
8	10	41
9	10.5	42
10	11	43
11	12	44
12	13	45

More useful conversions

1 centimetre	0.39 inches	1 inch	2.54 centimetres
1 metre	1.09 yards	1 yard	0.91 metres
1 kilometre	0.62 miles	1 mile	1. 61 kilometres
1 litre	1.76 pints	1 pint	0.57 litres
1 gram	0.035 ounces	1 ounce	28.35 grams
1 kilogram	2.2 pounds	1 pound	0.45 kilograms

This guide was written by **Katherine Vanderhaeghe**
Translated by **Trista Selous**
Project manager and copy editor **Margaret Rocques**
Series editor **Liz Coghill**
Additional research and assistance: Jenny Piening, Dave McCourt, Bernice Nikijuluw and Christine Bell

We have done our best to ensure the accuracy of the information contained in this guide. However, addresses, phone numbers, opening times etc. inevitably do change from time to time, so if you find a discrepancy please do let us know. You can contact us at: hachetteuk@orionbooks.co.uk or write to us at Hachette UK, address below.

Hachette UK guides provide independent advice. The authors and compilers do not accept any remuneration for the inclusion of any addresses in these guides.

Please note that we cannot accept any responsibility for any loss, injury or inconvenience sustained by anyone as a result of any information or advice contained in this guide.

Photo acknowledgements

Inside pages
Laurent Parrault : pp. 3 (t.r., c.), 10 (c., c.r.), 12 (c.r.), 13 (t.r., b.), 14, 15 (t., c. front, c. back), 16 (t., b.r.), 17 (t.r., b.), 18 (t.), 19 (t. l., c.r., b.r.), 20 (t., b.), 21 (t.r., c.l., b.r. , b.), 22 (t., b.), 23 (c.), 24, 25, 26 (c.), 27 (t., b. l.), 28 (t., b.), 30, 31, 36 (b.l.), 37, 38, 39, 40, 41, 43, 44, 45 (t., c.r., b.l.), 46, 47 (t.c., b.r.), 48, 49, 50, 51 (c.l., c.r. front, c.r. back, b.r.), 52, 53 (t.c., c.c., b.r.), 54 (b.l.), 55 (t.l., c.c., c.l., b.r.), 56, 58 (c.r., b.r.), 59, 60 (b.l.), 61 (t., b.l., b.r.), 62 (c.r.), 63, 64, 65 (t.l., t.r., t.c., b.l.), 66 (b.l.), 67, 69 (t.r.), 74 (b.l.), 75 (t.), 76 (b.r.), 78 (b.l.), 79 (t.r., b.l.), 84, 85, 86, 87 (b.r.), 88, 89 (t.c., t.r., b.r.), 90, 91, 92 (t., b.), 93, 94 (c.l., b.l.), 95, 96, 97 (b.r., c.c., c.r.), 98, 99 (c., b.), 100, 101, 102, 103, 104 (b.c., b.r.), 105 (c. l.), 106, 107 (t., c.r, b.l, b.r), 108 (t., b.), 109 (c.), 110 (t., b.c.), 111 (t., b.), 112, 113 (c.r.), 116 (t.l.), 117, 119 (b.r.), 120 (t.l.), 122.; **Christian Sarramon** : pp. 2 (t.), 3 (c., b.), 12 (t., b.), 13 (c.l.), 16 (c.r.), 17 (c.r.), 18 (c.r., b.l.), 19 (t.c.), 20 (c.r.), 22 (c.), 23 (c.r.), 26 (t.r.), 27 (c.l., c.r.), 28 (c.r.), 29 (t l., c l.), 36 (b.r.), 41 (c r. front), 51 (t.c.), 54 (c.r., b.r.), 57 (t r., b.l.), 58 (b l.), 62 (b l.), 70 (c.r.), 73 (t.), 78 (c.r.), 99 (t r.), 104 (c.r.), 105 (b.r.), 107 (c.c.), 108 (c.l.), 109 (t.l., t r., b.), 110 (c.r.), 111 (c.r.), 116 (b r.), 118, 119 (t l., c.l.); **Katherine Vanderhaeghe** : p. 17 (t.), p. 53 (c.l.), p. 89 (c.r.); **Éric Guillot** : p. 113 (t.c.); **Hachette** : pp. 10 (t., b.), 11 (t l., c.c., c r.), 13 (t. c., ©), 15 (b.l.), 21 (b.l.) , 45 (c.c.), 60 (c.r.), 61 (c.l., ©); **Riviera** : p. 57 (t.); **De Gouden Reael** : p. 65; **Canal House** : p. 71 (c.l.); **Ambassade Hotel** : p. 71 (b.r.); **Toro Hotel** : p. 73 (b.); **De Roode Leeuw** : p. 74 (c.l.); **Lonny's** : pp. 74 (b.), 75 (ht.); **Le Pêcheur** : p. 76 (c.l.); **Le Garage** : p. 77 (c.c.); **Zabar's** : p. 77 (b.r.); **The Pancake Bakery** : p. 78 (t.); **De Admiraal** : p. 79 (c.c.); **Van Heek** : p. 86 (b.r.); **Riviera** : p. 92 (c.); **Baobab** : p. 94 (c.r); **Kashba** : p. 94 (b.r.); **Nieuws** : p. 97 (t.r.); **Maranon** : p. 99 (t.l.); **Smokiana** : p. 105 (t.c. , c.c.); **Diva** : p. 111 (t.c.); **Second Best** : p. 113 (b.r.).

Front cover
Image Bank– Bokelberg : t.c.; **Image Bank–David de Lossy** : b.c.; **Christian Sarramon** : c.l., c.c., c.r., br.; **Laurent Parrault** : t.l., b.l.; **Pix V.C.L.** : c. r (figure).

Back cover
Christian Sarramon : t.r., c.l.; **Laurent Parrault** : c. (plate), b.l.

Illustrations: Pascal Garnier

Cartography © Hachette Tourisme

First published in the United Kingdom in 2000 by Hachette UK

© English Translation, revised and updated, Hachette UK 2000
© Hachette Livre (Hachette Tourisme) 1998

Distributed in the United States of America by Sterling Publishing Co., Inc.
387 Park Avenue South, New York, NY 10016-8810

A CIP catalogue for this book is available from the British Library

ISBN 184202 002 1

Hachette UK, Cassell & Co., The Orion Publishing Group, Wellington House, 125 Strand, London WC2R 0BB

Printed and bound in Italy

If you're staying for a few days and would like to try some new places, the following pages give you a wide choice of hotels, restaurants and bars, listed by district with addresses.
Although you can just turn up at a restaurant and have a meal (except in the most prestigious establishments), don't forget to book your hotel several days in advance (see page 68).
Enjoy your stay!

STAYING ON
A LITTLE LONGER

The prices quoted here are for a double room with en-suite bathroom or shower and include breakfast and local tax at 5%, but are a guide only. It's useful to know that in four and five-star hotels breakfasts are quite expensive (30–35Fl), but it's possible to book a room exclusive of breakfast. Prices shown are those that apply in high season though they may be subject to increases or reductions. It's also useful to know that many of the luxury hotels used by businessmen during the week reduce their charges at weekends. If you'd like to stay in an old-style hotel, make sure you book at least two months in advance.

For more detailed information see Rooms and Restaurants (p. 68).

Centraal Station

Golden Tulip Barbizon Palace*****
Prins Hendrikkade, 59-72
☎ 556 45 64
F 624 33 53
Around 470Fl.
A modern hotel, with an international clientele, occupying a group of 17th-century houses on the edge of the red light district. There's a conference room in the St. Olof Chapel and the restaurant has been awarded stars, but the rooms vary greatly. The ones in the old houses are preferable as they're better equipped and have views over the IJ. Perfect service.

Renaissance*****
Kattengat, 1
☎ 621 22 23
F 627 52 45
Around 580Fl.
An extremely large hotel complex (405 rooms), with an international clientele, and

including a 'brown café', disco, several restaurants and even a Lutheran church. Benefits from a very central location. Car park for patrons.

Victoria****
Damrak, 1-5
☎ 623 42 55/627 11 66
F 625 29 97/627 42 59
Around 485Fl.
A neo-Classical luxury hotel opposite the station, dating from 1890, with 305 huge, luxurious rooms, all double-glazed. Attractions include beautiful marble, stained-glass windows, a covered terrace with panoramic view and a fitness centre with swimming-pool and sauna.

Amstel Botel***
Oosterdokskade, 2-4
☎ 626 42 47
F 639 19 52
A large white ship moored near the central station, with 176 rather narrow but well-equipped cabins at reasonable prices. An unusual way to stay in the midst of Amsterdam's houseboats. Ask for a cabin overlooking the IJ because the quayside view isn't great.

Dam

Krasnapolsky*****
Dam, 9 (trams 4-9-16-20)
☎ 554 91 11
F 622 86 07
Around 660Fl.
Magnificent 19th-century hotel opposite the royal palace, with an immense garden where meals are served any time of day. Boasts 429 luxury rooms and a car park with 150 places, which is very useful in this district.

Amsterdam****
Damrak, 93-94 (trams 4-9-16-20)
☎ 555 06 66
F 620 47 16
Around 325Fl.
One of Amsterdam's old hotels near the Dam, now entirely renovated by the Best Western chain. Very good value for money and the restaurant serving Dutch specialities De Rode Leeuw on the ground floor won the Neerlands Dis prize.

Die Port van Cleve****
Nieuwezijds Voorburgwal, 176-180 (trams 1-2-5)
☎ 624 48 60
F 622 02 40
Around 360Fl.
Located behind the royal palace and the Magna Plaza shopping centre, this hotel is worth rediscovering, particularly since the renovation of its brasserie de Poort, serving authentic Dutch cuisine. The rooms have also been modernised.

Rembrandt Residence***
Herengracht, 255 (trams 13-17-20)
☎ 622 17 27
F 625 06 30
Around 295Fl.
A very cosy hotel occupying a group of 17th and 18th-century houses and admirably situated on the magnificent Herengracht, between Jordaan and the Dam. One of the best hotels in Amsterdam for those who want luxury hotel service at an affordable price.

Rho***
Nes, 11-23
☎ 620 73 71
F 620 78 26
Around 230Fl.
Sadly the conversion of the old Art Deco theatre does not extend beyond the vast foyer. The best of the 160 functionally-furnished rooms are at the back. Use of private car park for an additional charge.

The Béguinage c./Rokin

Doelen****
Nieuwe Doelenstraat, 24 (trams 4-9-16-20)
☎ 554 06 00
F 622 10 84
Around 455Fl.
One of the city's oldest hotels, where Sissi and Sarah Bernhardt stayed. The rooms are a little disappointing but the breakfast room overlooking the Amstel and the Belle Époque lounges are lovely. The best rooms (some with balconies) are at the back on the first and second floors.

Cok City***
Nieuwezijds Voorburgwal,
50 (trams 1-2-5)
☎ 422 00 11
🅵 420 03 57
Around 265Fl.
*Modernism and functionalism
are the watchwords in this hotel,
which has a lovely coloured
façade. Close to the university
and Spui, good value for money
for those who don't like
guesthouses.*

Nes***
Kloveniersburgwal,
137-139 (trams 4-9-
16-20)
☎ 624 47 73
🅵 620 98 42
Around 295Fl.
*A lovely Baroque gabled façade
hides this little hotel by the side
of a quiet canal behind Doelen.
Its 36 rooms have recently been
renovated and furnished with
every convenience. Ask for a
view over the Amstel. The
restaurants and bars of
Rembrandtplein are 5 mins
walk away.*

Rokin*
Rokin, 73 (trams 4-9-
16-20)
☎ 626 74 56
🅵 625 64 53
Around 180Fl.
*Very small and basic, but nice.
About half the rooms have
en-suite bathrooms or a view of
the canal. Usually a fairly young
clientele.*

Rembrandtplein

Schiller****
Rembrandtplein, 26-36
(trams 4-9)
☎ 554 07 00
🅵 624 00 98
Around 455Fl.
*This Art Deco gem, restored in
1997, has at last regained the
brilliance it had when it was first
built in 1912 by Fritz Schiller, an
amateur painter and art lover.
Cosy lounges, 92 tastefully
decorated rooms and a superb
brasserie which is one of the
favourite meeting-places of
Amsterdam's high society.*

Jolly Hotel Carlton****
Vijzelstraat, 4 (trams 16-
24-25)
☎ 622 22 66

🅵 626 61 83
Around 430Fl.
*Italian-style hospitality in this
fine brick building overlooking
Munttoren with Murano lights,
marble and designer furniture.
Good food and comfortable
rooms with en-suite bathrooms,
some with a lovely view.
Additional charge for use of
the garage.*

Canal Crown****
Herengracht, 519-525
(trams 16-24-25)
☎ 420 00 55
🅵 420 09 93
Around 350Fl.
*This hotel on the corner of
Vijzelstraat and Herengracht was
renovated throughout in 1993. It
has 56 very pleasant rooms with
lovely en-suite bathrooms.
Double glazing guarantees quiet
nights. Perfect service and a
24-hour bar.*

Eden***
Amstel, 144 (trams 9-20)
☎ 530 78 78
🅵 623 32 67
Around 275Fl.
*A small hotel by the Amstel,
managed by Best Western, very
modern but tastefully decorated.
The rooms overlooking the
Amstel have a magnificent view
but are a little more expensive.*

Amsterdam
Prinsengracht***
Prinsengracht, 1015
(trams 4-20)
☎ 623 77 79
🅵 623 89 26
Around 245Fl.
*A comfortable hotel not far from
the Van Loon museum, in the
'bourgeois' district of
Prinsengracht. There's a small
garden at the back and all
rooms are provided with en-
suite shower and toilet.*

Mercure Arthur
Frommer***
Noorderstraat, 46 (trams
16 -24-25)
☎ 622 03 28
🅵 620 32 08
Around 275Fl.
*The rooms are comfortable but
a little cramped and the
breakfast room is rather dark,
but the hotel benefits from a
quiet location and has a very
reasonably-priced car park.*

Ten minutes walk from the district with the best clubs in Amsterdam and the flower market.

Leidseplein

Maas***
Leidsekade, 91 (trams 1-2-5)
☎ 623 38 68
F 622 26 13
Around 350Fl.
A small, comfortable hotel not far from the large museums and the bustle of Leidseplein. It has some lovely rooms overlooking the canal. You will also enjoy the water beds and whirlpools. Baby-sitting service and generous breakfast.

Terdam***
Tesselschadestraat, 23 (trams 1-2-5)
☎ 612 68 76
F 683 83 13
Around 275Fl.
Although the Viennese decor is confined to the lobby, this is a pleasant hotel, well located in a comparatively quiet street for the district. And nobody will be jealous because the rooms are all the same.

Nieuwmarkt

The Grand*****
Oudezijds Voorburgwal, 197 (trams 4-9-16-20)
☎ 555 31 11
F 555 32 22
Around 800Fl.
In the 16th century this former city hall of Amsterdam was a royal residence, now converted into a luxury hotel ideally located in the heart of the city. After a day's sightseeing you'll appreciate the heated pool, sauna and Turkish bath. Private car park and a good brasserie.

Plantage

Lancaster***
Plantage Middenlaan, 48 (trams 9-14)
☎ 626 65 44
F 622 66 28
Around 220Fl.
This hotel opposite the Artis zoo has 88 comfortable rooms though with unoriginal decoration. Guests tend to be young and international.

Rembrandt**
Plantage Middenlaan, 17 (trams 9-14)
☎ 627 27 14
F 638 02 93
Around 155Fl.
This guesthouse in a 19th-century patrician house in a very green district is a stone's throw from Waterlooplein. Ideal for those on low budgets and families (rooms with 4 beds). Of the 16 rooms only 9 have en-suite shower and toilet. Those overlooking the garden are quieter.

The museum quarter

The Park***
Stadhouderskade, 25 (trams 6-7-10)
☎ 671 12 22
F 664 94 55
Around 350Fl.
This hotel offers 4-star service at affordable prices, with pretty, very comfortable rooms and a central location near the Rijksmuseum, sight-seeing boats and antique shops. Private car park.

Fita***
Jan Luykenstraat, 37 (trams 2-5-20)
☎ 679 09 76
F 664 39 69
Around 220Fl.
A quiet little hotel run by a nice couple. Sixteen large, light rooms with the latest in en-suite bathrooms, and a breakfast room in the basement. There are parking facilities in the area.

Aalders***
Jan Luykenstraat, 13-15 (trams 2-5-20)
☎ 673 40 27
F 673 46 98
Around 225Fl.
A favourite hotel for music-lovers because of its proximity to the Concertgebouw and museums. There's a very pleasant breakfast room, the bedrooms are light and spacious and the welcome is excellent.

Acro**
Jan Luykenstraat, 44 (trams 2-5-20)
☎ 662 55 38

F 675 08 11
Around 155Fl.
Two early 20th-century houses in a residential district a stone's throw from Vondelpark, the large museums and shopping streets have been converted into a functional hotel offering comfortable rooms at a very reasonable price.

De Pijp

Le Méridien Apollo****
Apollolaan, 2 (tram 25)
☎ 673 59 22
F 570 57 44
Around 550Fl.
If you prefer to explore Amsterdam by day rather than at night, you'll appreciate the quiet location of this modern hotel located on the Amstel, but some way from the centre. A good quality restaurant, generous breakfasts and a vast car park (for an additional charge).

La Richelle***
Holbeinstraat, 41 (trams 5-24)
☎ 671 79 71
F 671 05 41
Around 320Fl.
Although it's some way from the centre, this little hotel will please those who like a family welcome and beautiful location. Spacious rooms (some duplexes), light colours, antiques, Persian carpets and a small, typically Dutch garden full of flowers. Private car park for an additional charge and it's also possible to park in the street.

Don't forget to see pages 70–73 for more hotels.

HOTELS

Generally speaking, the Dutch eat dinner early. Restaurants open from 6pm and kitchens tend to close around 10pm. Prices shown here are a guide only but include 15% service.
For more information about opening hours, booking and prices, see Rooms and Restaurants Practicalities (p. 69).

Centraal Station

Lana-Thai
Warmoesstraat, 10
☎ 624 21 79
Open every day 5–11pm
Set meals 50–100Fl.
Stunning decor, including furniture and rich fabrics imported from Thailand, which fits perfectly with the authentic, highly-spiced cuisine. Don't miss the green curry and penang kung.

Vermeer
Prins Hendrikkade, 59-72
☎ 556 45 64
Open every day 6–11pm
Set meal 95Fl.
Truly excellent food, cosy decor and perfect service. The highly inventive, exclusively French cuisine is accompanied by carefully selected wines. Booking advisable. Free parking.

Dam

Brasserie Reflet
Hotel Krasnapolsky
Dam, 9
☎ 554 91 11
Open every day 6–11pm
Set meal 47.50Fl.
The superb Belle Époque decor, with its mirrors, stucco and palms, is not the only reason for coming here. The restaurant serves very tasty Mediterranean cuisine and the dessert trolley is breathtaking.

Dorrius
Nieuwezijds Voorburgwal, 5
☎ 420 22 24
Open every day 5.30–11pm.
Dark wood panelling on the walls and ceiling, tiles out of a painting by Vermeer, old stained-glass windows and moulded glass light fittings. This historic restaurant, dating from 1890 and renovated at last, serves authentic Dutch cuisine. Each month a different province comes under the spotlight, so you might find mussels from Zeeland, asparagus from Limburg or pheasant from the east. Succulent dishes served in regional crockery.

Lieve
Herengracht, 88
☎ 624 96 35
Open every day 6–10.30pm
Set meal 42.50Fl.
Fish specialities and some meat dishes, particularly game in season, cooked in the best tradition of Belgian gastronomy, inspired by Pierre Wijnants. A very popular place, no doubt because of its unforgettable shrimp croquettes and crab bisque. And as an accompaniment, one of the fine wines on the list, or perhaps one of the robust beers.

Jordaan

Cervejaria Alcantara
Westerstraat, 184-186
☎ 420 39 59
Open every day 6–11pm
From 30Fl. (no credit cards).
The setting is like a fish market, with bright light and the kitchen in the restaurant. Here you can sample enhanced Portuguese cuisine. This place is still very trendy and therefore busy.

Cilubang
Runstraat, 10
☎ 626 97 55
Open every day 6–11pm
Set meal 45Fl.
If you like to pick at lots of different dishes at once and truly love Indonesian food, go and order a rijsttaffel in this little restaurant that doesn't look like very much, but where the food is succulent.

Duende
Lindengracht, 62
☎ 420 66 92
Open every day 4pm–1am, Fri.–Sat. until 3am
Tapas 5–8.50Fl.
More than a tapas bar, a little restaurant decorated with Andalusian ceramics. Hard to choose between the 17 different tapas dishes, not including dishes of the day, all washed down with a robust Spanish wine. Flamenco show at the back once a month and live music every Saturday.

Koevoet
Lindenstraat, 17
☎ 624 08 46
Open every day 6–11pm
Set meal 40Fl.
A little workers' restaurant almost unchanged since 1850, with simple food, a convivial ambiance and house wine. Nothing extraordinary about the food, but enjoy the slice of Jordaan life.

Sancerre
Reestraat, 28-32
☎ 627 87 94
Open every day 6–10.30pm
Set meal 58Fl.
French cuisine with herbs, wines from the Loire, fine Art Deco interior and perfect service. A high-quality restaurant, competitively priced. Vegetarian dishes available.

Takens
Runstrat, 17d
☎ 627 06 18
Open every day 6–11pm; Sun. 11.30am–2.30pm
Set meals from 33.50Fl.
Edwin Takens loves subtle food, combining tastes and trends with a few exotic touches. Don't miss the shrimp bouillon with truffles or grilled steak with smoked oysters. Yet more surprises in the 6 set meals, which change weekly, and excellent wines.

Spui

D'Vijff Vlieghen
Spuistraat, 294-302
☎ 624 83 64
Open every day 5.30–10.30pm
Set meal 55Fl.
The decor hasn't changed for three hundred and fifty years, with gilded wallpaper, carved oak panelling and a labyrinth of cosy rooms where you can eat Dutch

nouvelle cuisine based on fish, seafood and vegetables in season.

Luden
Spuistraat, 304-306
☎ 622 89 79
Open every day
6pm–1am
Set meal from 42.50Fl.
A Parisian-style brasserie of the kind Amsterdammers love, the more so since it's one of the few restaurants with two sittings, at 6 and 9pm. Good if unsurprising, French-inspired food. Always packed, especially at weekends.

Leidseplein

Raffle's steakhouse
Kleine Gartmanplantsoen, 5
☎ 638 72 20
Open every day
5–11.30pm
Dishes 10–20Fl.
Warm Latin-American decor in blues and browns for lovers of good, charcoal-grilled Argentinian meat. BBQs, spare ribs, 500g/1lb steaks for the hungry, and empanadas and fish in season. Try the Uruguayan-style mussels and Chilean and Argentinian wines.

't Swarte Schaep
Korte Leidsedwarsstraat, 24
☎ 622 30 21
Open every day midday and evening
Set meals 50 and 90Fl.
Buried among the fast food outlets, this traditional restaurant is on the first floor of a house dating from 1687. Black pudding, lobster and good wines. A little expensive, but very good quality.

De Oesterbar
Leidseplein, 10
☎ 626 34 63
Open every day midday and evening
From 20Fl.
If you like fish, you'll love this restaurant entirely dedicated to the sea. Maatjes (marinated herrings) with onions, shrimps, oysters and eels, which you can eat at the bar at the back, or bigger dishes to eat round the table with a glass of iced jenever.

Rembrandtplein

Les Quatre Canetons
Prinsengracht, 1111
☎ 624 63 07
Mon.–Fri. lunch and dinner, Sat. dinner only
Set meals 57 and 82Fl.
As its French name suggests, this is the place to eat duck, duck with red peppers, foie gras and many other recipes invented by Jacques Roosebrand, who loves the food of south-west France. Good wine list.

Kort
Amstelveld, 12
☎ 626 11 99
Open every day
11.30am–midnight.
Set meal 50Fl.
Jim Kort opened his restaurant in the basement of the oldest wooden church in Amsterdam. Post-modern decor, French nouvelle cuisine and trendy clientele. When the sun shines they put out tables under the walnut trees on the charming little square.

Panini
Vijzelgrachr, 3-5
☎ 626 49 39
Open every day
noon–11pm
Dishes from 14.50Fl.
A lunchtime snack of Tuscan panini and salad or a more relaxed evening meal of fresh pasta, gamberetti and escalopes, washed down with a glass of chianti. Even with no sun you'll think you're in Italy as the ingredients and cuisine are 100% Italian.

Piet de Leeuw
Noorderstraat, 11
☎ 623 71 81
Open every day
noon–11pm, no lunch Sat. and Sun.
Dishes from 25Fl.
A typically Dutch restaurant frequented mainly by locals who eat good grilled steak, fresh sole or eels on toast at large buffet tables. Conviviality guaranteed.

RESTAURANTS

De Pijp

Quinto
Frans Halsstraat, 42
☎ 679 68 48
Open every day 6–11pm
Dishes from 20Fl.
If you're staying in this rather distant district of Amsterdam, you'll be very pleased to find this authentic café-restaurant with its warm decor of wood. Large convivial tables and a fairly limited menu that's full of great surprises. As well as the traditional hutspot you'll find ostrich and exotic fish. Besides which, it's a really friendly place.

Further afield

Amsterdam
Watertorenplein, 6
(terminus of tram 10)
☎ 682 26 66
Open every day
11.30am–11.30pm
Dishes from 19Fl.
The trendy new brasserie you mustn't miss, in a vast warehouse lit by big lights from the old Ajax stadium. Large and small meals all day, good wines, a good ambiance and good prices. Essential.

La Rive (Hotel Amstel)
Prof Tulpplein, 1 (trams 6-7-10)
☎ 622 60 60
Open every day
11.30am–11pm, no lunch
Sat. and Sun.
Certainly expensive, but succulent and unforgettable. If you want to treat yourself to a real gourmet meal, don't miss this truly wonderful restaurant overlooking the Amstel, particularly in summer when the terrace is open.

CAFÉ-RESTAURANTS

Centraal Station

New Deli
Haarlemmerstraat, 73
☎ 626 27 55
Open every day 10am–10pm
From 5.25Fl.
Chrome and primary colours. A designer setting for your Italian espresso and focaccio, sushi or Dutch rolls. Simple and good.

Nieuwmarkt

Dantzig
Zwanenburgwal, 15
☎ 620 90 41
Open every day
9am–1am.
Before or after your visit to the next-door Stopera, the largest terrace in town, by the side of the Amstel, and a wide range of large and small dishes at very affordable prices. Smart decor, mixed clientele.

In de Waag
Nieuwmarkt, 4
☎ 422 77 72
Open every day
10am–1am.
In the very fine, spare setting of the old St. Anthony dock you can lunch with the dish of the day, dine by candlelight with something more, or just have a real espresso. A truly exceptional terrace on a square in one of the nicest districts of Amsterdam.

Dam

Het Paleis
Paleisstraat, 16
☎ 626 06 00
Open every day
11am–1am and 2am
Fri. and Sat.
In this café close to the palace, Inge and Babette will give you a royal reception, whether it's for a quick snack or a slow drink. In summer the large terrace by the water's edge is fit for a king.

Villa Zeezicht
Torensteeg, 7
Open every day
8am–7pm, 9am–7pm at weekends.
At this café, with its superb view of one of the city's largest bridges and its tables outside in fine weather, you can have cakes or savoury snacks, tea and Italian coffee. Service provided entirely by women, all very nice and friendly.

Jordaan

Café Nielsen
Berenstraat, 29
☎ 624 42 98
Tue.–Sat. 8.30am–5pm,
Sun. 9.30am–5pm.
For those who'd rather have their breakfast or brunch in a café than at the hotel, real Italian coffee broodjes (rolls), lovely salads and home-made tarts, all served by a very friendly couple.

Leidseplein

American Café
Leidsekade, 97
☎ 624 53 22
Open every day
10am–1am, brunch from 11.30am.
This Art Deco café lit by magnificent period Tiffany lamps is still one of the pleasantest places in Amsterdam to drink a coffee while reading the paper, eat a hamburger or curry, or have brunch on Sundays to the sound of live jazz.

Don't forget to look on pages 123–124 for restaurant vocabulary and menu translator.

RESTAURANTS

Young people in Amsterdam meet up in cafés and bars before setting off to dance the night away in clubs. For more information on what to wear and opening hours, turn to Nightlife Practicalities (see pages 114-115).

BARS-CAFÉS

Centraal Station

Latei
Zeedijk, 143
☎ 625 74 85
Mon.-Sat. 8am-5pm
If you're desperate to take home the crockery your breakfast was served on, no problem, you can have it for a few florins, because everything's for sale here, including the furniture. But don't let that stop you finishing your delicious apple tart.

Vol Zee café
Prins Hendrikkade, 94-95
☎ 543 47 36
Mon.-Thu. 10am-1am,
Fri.-Sat. 10am-3am,
Sun. 11am-1am.
The tower of weeping women overlooking the Oosterdok, from where the ships used to set sail on dangerous voyages, has become a nice, friendly café full of crimson velvet and much more laughter and drinking than weeping and wailing.

Mooy
Kolksteeg,12
☎ 624 02 94
Open every day
noon-1am.
Mooy has been here since 1620 and is still going strong among the local sex shops and dens of ill repute. It has a traditional Amsterdam café decor of Delft tiles, copper light fittings and a rather old-fashioned air, which also applies to some of the customers.

Dam

Ter Kuile
Torensteeg, 8-8
☎ 639 10 55
Open every day
11am-1am.

A new generation 'brown café' with Art Deco lamps and lovely wrought iron, frequented by the young and hip or laid back in a nice part of town between Dam and Jordaan. Snacks and light meals served all day.

Leidseplein

Het Hok
Lange Leidsedwarsstraat, 134
☎ 624 31 33
Open every day until 1am.
Cosy ambiance and maximum concentration around the chess board. A locals' café where, despite the mental battles at hand, they don't forget to raise their glasses or laugh and talk between games.

Spui

Café Gollem
Raamsteeg, 4
Open every day
10am-1am.
The café for lovers of Belgian beer, with nine different draught beers and 200 bottled varieties available.

De Still
Spuistraat, 326
☎ 620 13 49
Open every day
5pm-1am.
A pub-style café specialising in whisky. An unbelievable choice of blends and malts from around the world, including Japan. A great place to meet before or after dinner.

Jordaan

Café Tabac
Brouwersgracht, 101
(corner of Prinsengracht)
☎ 622 44 13
Open every day
11am-1am, Fri. and Sat.
until 3am
Wooden benches and bar, tobacco coloured walls, quiet and cosy during the day, very busy at night. Here you can have a late breakfast, a good draught beer or sit outside for a drink before dinner in summer.

De Koophandel
Bloemgracht, 49
Sun.-Thu. 10pm-3am,
Fri.-Sat. 10pm-4am.

This café housed in a former Jordaan warehouse is also a meeting place where occasional exhibitions are held. Live music at weekends and snacks and light meals all day long.

Thijssen
Brouwersgracht, 107
(corner of Lindengracht)
☎ 623 89 94
Mon.-Fri. 9am-1am, Sat.
7am-2.30am.
This new generation 'brown café' near Noordermarkt, larger and with a more designer look than the older ones, is decorated with magnificent Art Deco lamps. Very busy on Saturdays, which is market day, and Friday nights. Wide choice of delicious rolls served during the day.

Rembrandtplein

Planet Hollywood
Reguliersbreestraat, 35
☎ 427 78 27
Open every day
noon-2am.
Bruce, Sylvester and Arnold have finally landed in Amsterdam among the sex shops and peep shows. Giant screen, hamburgers, T-shirts, milk shakes and all kinds of cocktails. For seeing and being seen.

See page 120 for more late night cafés and bars.

NIGHTCLUBS

The Supperclub
Jonge Roelensteeg, 21
Wed.–Sun. 7pm–2/3am.
The latest, hippest pre-club bar in a dark little street near the Dam, where you can eat or drink to sounds mixed by the best DJs. An essential stop before you dive into one of Amsterdam's hottest clubs.

Sinners in Heaven
Wagenstraat, 3-7
(Plantage)
Thu.–Sun. 10pm–2/3am.
The new temple of dance and glamour on 3 floors with 3 different ambiances: church, chateau or dungeon. Special sinners' night every Sunday.

Margarita's
Regulierdwarsstraat,
108-114
Wed.–Sun. 9pm–2/3am.
Black magic vinyl groove with a dash of Latino. Dance to Caribbean rhythms on Saturday, salsa on Sunday.

Dansen bij Jansen
Handboogstraat, 11
☎ 620 17 79
Open every day
11pm–4am.
A disco purely for students, who dance the night away like maniacs to house music. Photos by the entrance give you an idea of how to dress to please the doorman. Not for over-25s.

Exit
Regulierdwarsstraat, 42
☎ 625 87 88
Open every day 7pm–
1/3am.
A very popular gay club. Great music for dancing.

Time
Nieuwezijds Voorburgwal,
163-5
Open Tue-Sun 10pm-4am
Admission 10Fl, free
before 11pm.
New, smart looking club with mirrors and a long bar which attracts a young crowd. Tuesday is reggae night, Wednesday is the popular drum and bass night. Rest of the week features house and dance music.

More
Rozengracht, 133
☎ 528 74 59
Open Wed.–Sun.
10pm–3/4am
Housed in the former Roothaanhuis, this bright club, with its white walls and pink floor, has plenty of room for dancing. Each week there's a different theme with house DJs and acts providing the entertainment. Every Wednesday night is gay night. Cover charge 15Fl.

Paradiso
details on page 121 and
De Melkweg
details on page 122
Although already featured on pages 121 and 122, we thought these two were worth a mention here, as their dance nights at the weekend are extremely popular and very trendy.

See pages 121–122 for more clubs and live music.

BARS/CLUBS

NOTES

NOTES

HACHETTE TRAVEL GUIDES

Titles available in this series:
A GREAT WEEKEND IN AMSTERDAM (ISBN: 1 84202 002 1)
A GREAT WEEKEND IN BARCELONA (ISBN: 1 84202 005 6)
A GREAT WEEKEND IN BERLIN (ISBN: 1 84202 061 7)
A GREAT WEEKEND IN BRUSSELS (ISBN: 1 84202 017 X)
A GREAT WEEKEND IN FLORENCE (ISBN: 1 84202 010 2)
A GREAT WEEKEND IN LISBON (ISBN: 1 84202 011 0)
A GREAT WEEKEND IN LONDON (ISBN: 1 84202 013 7)
A GREAT WEEKEND IN MADRID (ISBN: 1 84202 095 1)
A GREAT WEEKEND IN NAPLES (ISBN: 1 84202 016 1)
A GREAT WEEKEND IN NEW YORK (ISBN: 1 84202 004 8)
A GREAT WEEKEND IN PARIS (ISBN: 1 84202 001 3)
A GREAT WEEKEND IN PRAGUE (ISBN: 1 84202 000 5)
A GREAT WEEKEND IN ROME (ISBN: 1 84202 003 X)
A GREAT WEEKEND IN VENICE (ISBN: 1 84202 018 8)
A GREAT WEEKEND IN VIENNA (ISBN: 1 84202 026 9)

Coming soon:
A GREAT WEEKEND IN DUBLIN (ISBN: 1 84202 096 X)

HACHETTE VACANCES
Who better to write about France than the French?
A series of colourful, information-packed, leisure and activity guides for
family holidays by French authors. Literally hundreds of suggestions for
things to do and sights to see per title.

Titles available:
BRITTANY (ISBN: 1 84202 007 2)
DORDOGNE & PÉRIGORD (ISBN: 1 84202 098 6)
LANGUEDOC-ROUSSILLON (ISBN: 1 84202 008 0)
NORMANDY (ISBN: 1 84202 097 8)
POITOU-CHARENTES (ISBN: 1 84202 009 9)
PROVENCE & THE COTE D'AZUR (ISBN: 1 84202 006 4)
PYRENEES & GASCONY (ISBN: 1 84202 015 3)
SOUTH-WEST FRANCE (ISBN: 1 84202 014 5)

Coming soon:
CATALONIA (ISBN: 1 84202 099 4)
CORSICA (ISBN: 1 84202 100 1)

ROUTARD
Comprehensive and reliable guides offering insider advice for the
independent traveller.

Titles available:
CALIFORNIA, NEVADA & ARIZONA (ISBN: 1 84202 025 0)
IRELAND (ISBN: 1 84202 024 2)
PARIS (ISBN: 1 84202 027 7)
THAILAND (ISBN: 1 84202 029 3)

Coming soon:
BELGIUM (ISBN: 1 84202 022 6)
CUBA (ISBN: 1 84202 062 5)
GREEK ISLANDS & ATHENS (ISBN: 1 84202 023 4)
NORTHERN BRITTANY (ISBN: 1 84202 020 X)
PROVENCE & THE COTE D'AZUR (ISBN: 1 84202 019 6)
ROME & SOUTHERN ITALY (ISBN: 1 84202 021 8)
WEST CANADA & ONTARIO (ISBN: 1 84202 031 5)